Easter: Stories & More will enhance your understanding of what Jesus has done for us. Enter into the passion week of Christ with these well-written stories, devotionals, and poems.

— SIGMUND BROWER

Readers will be gripped by stories of the crucifixion, burial, and resurrection told from amazingly imaginative points of view—the priest discovering that the inches-thick curtain in front of the Holy of Holies was torn apart, the angel sent for a special task, the spike hammered through Jesus' hand.

"Oh this is good," I frequently said. "I wish I'd written that!"

— JACK POPJES, BIBLE TRANSLATOR & AUTHOR
WWW.JACKPOPJES.COM

Verna
from Sylvia
(page 9
page 20
page 107)

EASTER: STORIES & MORE

INSCRIBE CHRISTIAN WRITERS' FELLOWSHIP

InScribe Press

Paperback: 978-0-9940405-4-1

Ebook: 978-0-9940405-5-8

Edited by Pat Gerbrandt, Marcia Laycock, Kathleen Friesen, and Tracy Krauss.

Layout by Ruth L. Snyder

Cover Design by 99Designs

Printed in Canada by PageMaster Publishing

Dedication

This book is lovingly dedicated to Bobbi Junior who was a member and faithful executive member of InScribe Christian Writers' Fellowship for many years. She has set the bar high for those of us who follow in her footsteps.

Foreword

Easter commemorates the resurrection of our Lord Jesus Christ. As such, it is the pinnacle of the Christian year.

The apostle Paul insists that without the resurrection, Christians are to be most pitied amongst all people (1 Corinthians 15:19). Why? Because Christians talk a lot about how through the risen Jesus we can have our sins forgiven and be reconciled to God to receive eternal life. The logic is simple: if Jesus were not resurrected from the dead, then "our preaching is useless, and so is [our] faith" (1 Corinthians 15: 14).

The word Paul uses here for preaching is really just an everyday word for "announcement." Preaching isn't just what pastors do Sunday morning but is what every Christian does when we tell others something about Jesus. Thus, to paraphrase the apostle for today: If Easter is not true, then all our talk about Jesus is trivial at best, or deceptive at worst.

To put it bluntly, the authenticity and power of our words as Christians *utterly depends* on Jesus' resurrection from the dead.

Before Jesus ascended back to the right hand of the Father in heaven, he gave the apostles a simple but profound mandate: "You will be my witnesses," he said, "in Jerusalem, and in all Judea and Samaria, and to the ends of the earth" (Acts 1:9).

Be witnesses. That's the task Jesus delegates to us. Witnesses to the resurrected Jesus.

What do witnesses do? In a court of law, a witness is not called upon to prove a case. Fortunately, Jesus didn't call us to be prosecutors or defense lawyers. Rather, witnesses provide a sworn affidavit, an oral or written statement to what they have seen, heard and experienced. Not everyone may believe them, but their job is simply to testify to what they know to be true.

We realize, however, that witnesses do not see everything precisely the same. An accident at a busy intersection may be seen by many individuals and yet their account of what happened will vary. These variances shaped by their own memory, life experience, vantage point, vocabulary and experiences bring into sharper relief a fuller picture of what *really* happened. One witness is important, but multiple witnesses are exponentially compelling.

What does this all have to do with the chapters set out before you in this book? Let me suggest that these pieces are a collective of Easter witnesses. The authors represent a wide range of backgrounds, ages, experiences and perspectives, and the genres in which they write include devotionals, non-fiction, fiction, poetry, and even recipes. And yet each in their own creative and unique way are witnesses that expand the evidence for the reality of Easter.

A parenthetical note: I confess I wasn't sure what to do with the last section that includes Easter recipes. I thought I'd just conveniently ignore them in this foreword as not quite fitting into my designation of the authors as "witnesses" to Easter—until I remembered that Jesus prepared a meal of fish for his followers after his resurrection. Eating together with him was concrete evidence that he was bodily present, not just a ghost. And oh yes, he also instructed his followers that they should regularly commemorate his death with community meals. So, I happily conclude that the preparation and celebration of

Easter meals is one of the more joyous times when we witness to one another of our shared fellowship in and with our risen Lord. Let's eat!

I'm sure all the authors want you to appreciate the creative energy they've expended to write these pieces. By all means, drink deeply from these literary waters. But you will have forgone deeper nourishment if all you get is your literary thirst slaked.

Rather, be sure to wade deeper into spiritual waters by allowing the Spirit to use the testimony of each author as yet another faithful witness to the miracle of the risen Lord Jesus Christ. In this way, each chapter adds to an ever-growing cloud of witnesses proclaiming, "He is risen! He is risen indeed!"

-David Guretzki, PhD
Executive Vice President and Resident Theologian
The Evangelical Fellowship of Canada
Epiphany 2021

Introduction

How exciting to see another InScribe Anthology rolling off the presses! *Easter Stories & More* follows on the success of *Christmas Stories & More* and promises to be just as engaging and inspiring with stories, poems, devotionals—and more—written by InScribe members from across our country. It might seem like a natural progression to move from Christmas to Easter, but in fact, I would be remiss if I didn't thank a few people in particular.

It all started with some blog posts. Thanks to Sandi Somers' inspiring themes each month, contributors to our *InScribe Writers' Online* blog wrote pieces during Easter of 2019 from the point of view of those who may have been there during that first Easter. Contributions were so creative and from such a variety of viewpoints that it was one of our most successful and talked about online series. Alan Anderson, a long-time member of I*nScribe Christian Writers' Fellowship* and a regular contributor to our blog, suggested that these posts be collected and published. This was exactly the catalyst needed to spur the next InScribe Anthology to life. You can find most of these original stories in the Creative Non-Fiction section.

Thank you to the InScribe Press team of volunteers, starting with Press Coordinator, Ruth L. Snyder and team members Kathleen Friesen, Pat Gerbrandt, Marcia Laycock, Diane Welch, and Tracy Krauss who screened submissions, sent contracts, attended meetings, edited, proofread, formatted and did all the many other tasks necessary to take this Anthology from idea to reality. Of course, many other people also made contributions, but I can't possibly name them all. If you had a hand in making *Easter Stories & More* come to life, please accept my heartfelt thank-you!

You will find bios for many of the individual authors, all members of *InScribe Christian Writers' Fellowship*, at the back of the book. InScribe Press is a ministry of ICWF, a Canada-wide organization for writers of Christian faith whose mandate is to "minister to Canadian Christian writers by stimulating, supporting, and encouraging them in the advancement of their writing so they can effectively minister to others, promote Christianity, and contribute to the public's appreciation of the arts."

If you enjoy this book, please consider leaving a short book review online wherever books are sold. If you are a Canadian Christian writer, consider joining us: www.inscribe.org

Sincerely,
Tracy Krauss
President, InScribe Christian Writers' Fellowship

PART I
DEVOTIONALS

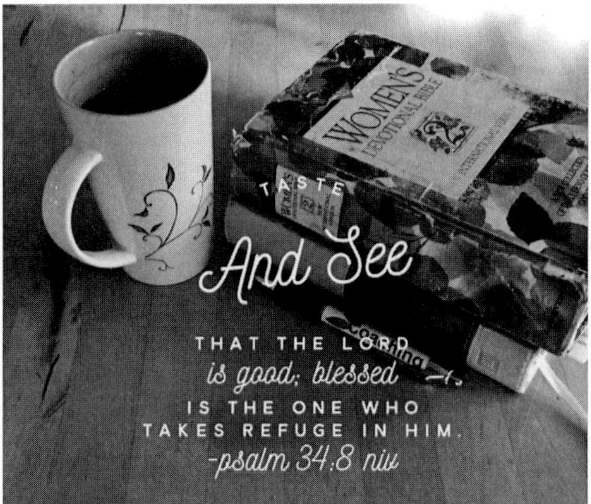

Photo by Ruth L. Snyder

Holy Week

BY MARNIE POHLMANN

Easter is the Christian celebration that goes from joy, "Hosanna," to despair, “Crucify Him”, to hope, "He is risen. He is risen indeed."

For some, the Easter period begins with Lent, a time of sacrifice and contemplation about what Jesus' sacrifice means to us. This tradition is an opportunity for us to examine ourselves and our need of a Saviour. Do you give up something for Lent and use the time to examine your life and your relationship with God?

After Lent comes Holy Week.

- *Sunday - Celebrating Jesus as King.*
- *Monday/Tuesday - Money changers. Teaching at the Temple.*
- *Wednesday - Judas is tempted.*
- *Thursday – Passover Feast*
- *Friday - “Crucify him,” “It is finished”*
- *Saturday – Silence.*
- *Sunday - “He is risen. He is risen indeed!”*

And Easter is complete. We go back to work, or school, or our families. We continue to gather at church services once a week to sing worship songs.

As I look at this holy week of events, I realize that if I missed contemplating my relationship with God through the time of Lent, or wish to continue that self-examination, here was another opportunity. I could take the events of each Holy Week day to ask questions about my own walk with Christ.

Sunday – Celebrating Jesus as King.

Am I following God to enjoy the good life of celebrations or am I a follower on the good days AND the bad days? Am I a Sunday-only Christian or is walking with God my way of life?

Monday/Tuesday – Money changers. Teaching at the Temple.

What does where I spend my money say about me? Does it show I am committed to God or that I am swayed by other things? These things may not be bad in themselves, and may be different for each person, but what are my priorities?

Am I learning and practicing what Scripture tells me? Am I gathering with other believers to ask questions, discuss Scripture, and test my beliefs?

Wednesday – Judas is tempted.

Do I know God or am I making God be who I want Him to be, taking the parts I want but rejecting the parts of God I am uncomfortable with? Am I following God or asking God to follow me in my desires? Do I make decisions first then ask for blessing and forgiveness, rather than trusting God to guide my life?

Thursday – Passover Feast.

Am I gathering with other believers? Am I serving them and serving with them, or only expecting them to serve me? Do I pray intimately with them or do I fall asleep? Do I take my own struggles to God and submit to His way?

Friday - "Crucify him," "It is finished"

When troubles come, do I stand true - even in times that hurt? Am I willing to suffer pain, abandonment, and rejection to follow God through to the end of this life?

Saturday – Silence.

Do I trust God in the silence or do I hide in fear? Do I wait in anticipation for His promises to be fulfilled in His time?

Sunday - "He is risen. He is risen indeed!"

Am I living in this physical time as though eternity and the Kingdom of God are at hand? What do I really believe about the resurrection?

Without restored life, I remain lost. Christ's death and resurrection for our salvation has been accomplished, but our own part in the Kingdom of God is not finished. **Christ is risen!** How do we answer these questions presented by the events of Holy Week?

- Am I a Palm Sunday "Hosanna" Christian?
- Am I a "Crucify him" Christian, depending on who I am with?
- Do I believe only to the point of the crucifixion death?
- Am I believer in "He is risen. He is risen indeed" and do I live like I believe this?

Easter, the Christian celebration, from joy to despair to hope. Will the choices I make in response to this Christian season continue in my life as a testimony to the redemption given by the *living* God?

Filthy Rags

BY CAROL HARRISON

I love to use object lessons when I speak at Bible camp. It helps grab the campers' attention and often increases understanding of the message. Evening chapel time arrived and I pulled all the pieces I needed out of my camp bag for an object lesson I had not tried before using it at camp. I hoped it worked the way I imagined.

The pristine, white cotton cloth had no spots, wrinkles, or tears. Then, I pulled out a bottle of iodine, which can stain our skin and anything it touches, brown. I reminded them of Romans 3: 23, "For all have sinned and fall short of the glory of God." Each time they named a sin, something that God says is wrong, I added a drop of Iodine onto the now folded white cloth. Just a dab to represent the ones they mentioned like lying, stealing, cheating, disobedience, fighting, bullying, and hurting others.

The cloth took on a brown polka dot appearance. As a volunteer opened up the folds, the campers saw how the one little sin dab had spread through the layers just like sin invades every part of us. Even what we might think is a small sin grows into a bigger mess.

The campers hollered about how I ruined my cloth. I agreed and grabbed a bowl from my bag and a bottle of water to fill it. I asked my leader volunteer to scrub the cloth while I kept sharing about how our lives are filled with sin. We think a little white lie is not too bad but God says it is no different than hitting someone. Anger is no different than murder. Sin is sin.

The campers listened and watched. The volunteer held up the cloth. No matter how hard he scrubbed it, it did not come clean. Instead it began to look like a filthy rag—even better than I expected. I told my helper to scrub harder. The water took on a brownish hue but the sin stains spread until the entire cloth contained shades of brown with no white left anywhere. We needed more help.

I offered another bowl of clean water but the helper and campers shook their heads and shouted how useless another bowl of water would be. Iodine sin stains had permanently ruined my cloth. I added bleach to the second bowl of water because we needed help. Isaiah 64:6 says, "All of us have become like one who is unclean, and all our righteous acts are like filthy rags."

We had a filthy rag that we had tried and tried to clean, only to make it worse. Acts 4:12 says, "Salvation is found in no one else, for there is no other name under heaven given to men by which we must be saved."

John 3: 16 says, "For God so loved the world that He gave His one and only son that whoever believes in him should not perish but have eternal life."

Romans 6:23 gave us a solution. "For the wages of sin is death but the gift of God is eternal life through Jesus Christ our Lord."

As we added the bleach to represent the blood Jesus shed for us on the cross, we added the power necessary to clean the filthy rag just like Jesus cleanses our sin-filled hearts. The campers watched in amazement as the bleach-water restored the cloth to its original white, unblemished form. Jesus can clean our hearts and lives to be right with God, who will look at us just as if we had never sinned. But the choice to accept his cleansing is ours to make.

His Supreme Sacrifice for Our Sins!

BY SYLVIA ENGEN ESPE

"When Christ came as high priest of the good things that are already here, he went through the greater and more perfect tabernacle that is not man-made, that is to say, not a part of this creation. He did not enter by the means of the blood of goats and calves, but he entered the Most Holy Place once for all by his own blood, having obtained eternal redemption" Hebrews 9:11-12 (NIV).

Crown of Thorns Photo by Kimberley Payne

I was awestruck! The crown of Thorns plant before me, grown in the shape of a crown, boasted brightly coloured flowers that were exquisite and delicate. This poisonous plant was named for a reason. The sharp thorns that grow on fleshy brown stems are wicked. According to a legend, a Crown of Thorns plant was given its name after it was associated with the crown of thorns placed on Jesus's head at the time of His crucifixion.* But the remarkable feature of this plant is that it blooms unceasingly.

Jesus paid the supreme sacrifice for our sins with His precious blood shed on the cross. Redemption refers to the process of freeing a slave, a person who was owned by someone else and could be bought or sold according to Old Testament laws. But God sent His Son to wear the crown of thorns, suffer, and die for our sins. He fulfilled the law in our stead once and for all. God's new covenant did away with the rules they practised in the Old Testament times, rules that insisted the high priest was the only one who could enter the Most Holy Place and offer sacrifices to atone for the sins of the people.

Christ's love and forgiveness are unceasing—just as the Crown of Thorns plant goes on blooming. May we obediently seek God's guidance to follow His specific leading each day. Perhaps the parents down the street who lost their only daughter, the Music Director of the church choir recently diagnosed with cancer, and the local Postmaster's son who expressed a desire to go to Sunday School require our love and prayerful involvement. We, too, can bloom unceasingly by His grace as do the blossoms on the Crown of Thorns plant.

Dear Lord, thank you for wearing a crown of thorns, and paying the supreme price for our redemption. Amen.

* John 19:2

Do the Math

BY MARNIE POHLMANN

I like to reconcile my bank accounts. To the penny. Every month. I also like to keep lists. A list of deadlines. A list of chores. A list of creative projects.

My penchant for math is helpful in my spiritual walk.

On the day between Good Friday and Easter Sunday, we remember how the body of Christ is enclosed in the tomb. The cross is empty. Yet the stone has not yet rolled away. So, we pause. That Saturday is the day of waiting.

For such a time as this, Jesus had counted the cost. His life balanced the need for a perfect sacrifice so we could be set free of the consequences of sin.

Celebrating Easter weekend, I can join in the waiting and the contemplation. I can count the cost of my belief. I can check the sin in my life to keep short accounts. I can balance my doing and my worship to become Christ-like in my walk. So, I pause. Selah. And I do the math.

Christ died so we can be fully reconciled to God. To the penny.
Always and forever.
Do the math.

It is Finished

BY MARNIE POHLMANN

I'm not sure I will ever say the words, "It is finished." Perhaps this is because I am a mother, familiar with this vocation that is never finished. Even when a chore is complete, a few hours later it is undone.

Parents spend time

making a meal that is eaten in ten minutes,

while soon everyone is hungry again…

washing the dishes,

to dirty them with another meal…

sweeping the floor,

only to have crumbs and dust bunnies multiply...

folding the laundry,

and seeing the same shirts end up back in the dirty clothes basket…

making beds,

then sending kids to them for a nap…

Everything done becomes undone. It never ends!

Because a mother's work is never finished.

And that's all right. We eventually come to be at peace with the undone.

"It is finished."

Even our Lord, who said these words as He died on the cross, wasn't really finished!

Jesus rose from the dead (Hallelujah!) so we can be God's work in progress.

Sometimes we rebel…

Sometimes we run…

Sometimes we laze about the house not helping with the chores…

And God continues to love, nurture, and grow us.

God is an expert on resurrection and new life. So, when we look at our parenting or our unfinished projects, we can be at peace.

God's work in us and through us is never finished.

A Bad Day and the Day After

BY MARCIA LEE LAYCOCK

My dog died yesterday. We got a call from the vet that she'd been hit by a car. She was still alive when we got there and we had to decide whether or not to try and keep her that way or not. She was an old dog – somewhere around eighteen, we think, and she was in pain, so we did what was merciful.

Then I got home to find an email from an editor saying he was rejecting a manuscript I'd sent him. The words took a while to sink in.

I was expecting my dog to die soon. She was very old. I was pretty sure that manuscript would be rejected by that editor. It isn't ready to be published. But it was still a bad day. A day when things die always is.

But now that the day is over and I look back on it, I see there were some good things in that space of twenty-four hours. I was able to put my hand over my dog's beating heart one more time and cry a little before having to go on with a day full of things that needed to be done. I was able to be thankful for the fifteen years that little ball of fur and bone was underfoot. I was able to be thankful for friends that make you feel better just by sitting across a table sipping tea; for days full of mundane things that are so beautiful in their rhythm that you hardly notice. And for that word, "hardly," because I did notice, just a bit; for the hope that gives me. And for editors whose rejections leave you still believing in the dreams you have for words strung across a page.

There are always things to be thankful for, even on a day when death becomes a reality. There is always hope for a new day, hope that the darkness won't always seem impenetrable.

There is always hope because our Redeemer lives. It was a dark day when He died—literally, according to the scriptures—but Jesus didn't stay wrapped in death. He rose and walked among his friends again, spoke to them, encouraged them, ate with them. He not only gave them hope for a new day, he gave them life forever after, life lived in the presence of God.

The Apostle John wrote that "Jesus did many other miraculous signs in the presence of his disciples, which are not recorded in this book. But these are written that you may believe that Jesus is the Christ, the son of God and that by believing you may have life in his name." (John 20:30,31).

We no longer live within the day on which death seemed victorious. We live in the day that came three days after. We call it Easter.

Jesus also said, "blessed are those who have not seen and yet have believed." (John 20:29b).

An Empty Tomb

BY LYNN J. SIMPSON

On the evening of that first day of the week, when the disciples were together, with the doors locked for fear of the Jewish leaders, Jesus came among them and said, "Peace be with you!" John 20:19

An empty tomb.

The tomb which had held Jesus, their Saviour, their teacher, their friend, was empty. The broken body of their King, gone.

Peter and John, along with the other disciples, (except for Judas who had betrayed Jesus, and for Thomas who was not with them that day) drew together behind a locked door. John's gospel teaches it was a first day of the week, and Peter and John had recently witnessed an empty tomb except for strips of linen, and the cloth that had been wrapped around Jesus' head.

An empty tomb.

Although scripture does not name the room where the disciples were hiding that day, bible scholars think it may have been the room upstairs where they stayed before (Act 1:13) and reference it as the Upper Room.

In the Upper Room that day, I imagine the disciples' fear and sadness laced the air, along with the lingering smell of bread and wine from their last supper when Jesus, their Saviour, their teacher, their friend was still there.

I imagine Peter feeling regret, the roosters crow still echoing in his mind.

I imagine John, tears flowing freely in grief and wondering how best to honour his Saviour's request to take care of Jesus' mother, Mary.

I imagine, even though they huddled together, the room felt empty without the presence of Jesus whose love they had known.

A love that now seemed gone, with an empty tomb while they huddled in that locked Upper Room.

And, I imagine, all the disciples hoping they could have just one more day with Him.

Then…

Then, He is suddenly standing before them!

"Peace be with you," He says.

Peace be with you.

Even after all He had endured—whippings, a crown of thorns, a cross to carry, nails in His hands, and all the sin of world upon Him…

His first words to His beloved disciples were to settle their grieving, fearful, and shameful hearts.

"Peace be with you!"

And "The disciples were overjoyed when they saw the Lord" John 20:20.

Even when all seems empty, gone—a loved one, a job, a dream, a friend, a child moving out, consequences from a mistake—and your heart is grieving, may you remember Jesus' first words to His disciples that day He appeared.

"Peace be with you."

Those words are for you too, today and forever more.

He is Risen

SYLVIA ENGEN ESPE

"Brothers, we do not want you to be ignorant about those who fall asleep, or grieve like the rest of men, who have no hope. We believe that Jesus died and rose again and so we believe that God will bring with Jesus those who have fallen asleep in him." 1 Thessalonians 4:13 (NIV)

"Daddy can't die yet," cried our nine-year-old daughter. "I didn't say goodbye to him!" It was on Maundy Thursday, the eve before Jesus's death on the cross, that God called a loving husband and father from his life here on earth. I remember my broken heart reminded me of the dark events that led to Good Friday. The death of a loved one taught me emphatically that life is brief, and fragile.

My mind drifted back to younger years when dreams excited me. I dreamed of a joyful future with a perfect family of my own. My dreams included a God-fearing prince to be at my side. "But dear Lord," I prayed, "I do not wish to marry a preacher." I had vivid memories of sad pastors' farewells in our Church. It wasn't easy to say goodbye to beloved pastors' families. However God did bless my life with the gift of love of a young pastor. My desires were no longer in conflict with God's will for my life. This miraculous gift of discovering the deep unity of heart and mind; the committed cooperation to become partners in love, became ours. God transformed a passing acquaintanceship into a lasting relationship.

My reverie finally brought me back to reality. I realized Easter is a time for me to reflect on the gift of life. My salvation cost God the life of His Son. I am reminded that in our dying world, God does bring life. God's Word tells me that only through God's power is life brought from death, and eternal victory is won. This victory is for all believers including Jim and me.

I claim the Words of our resurrected Lord that because He lives, we too shall live.* I can again rejoice in the resurrection. It proclaims to me that the finality of death is gone. It tells me that in Christ we shall all rise from the grave and live forever with Him. When Christ returns, all believers who are dead and alive will be reunited.

Dear Lord, thank you for the gift of life. Thank you for the gift of the Easter message which is a time to remember and rejoice. Thank you for dying on the cross, opening the doors to new life to all who accept You as their personal Saviour. You have risen! Amen.

* John 14:19 (NIV)

Risen with Christ

BY NORMAND ARSENEAULT

I struggled with understanding the crucified life until I discovered the second part of Galatians 2:20. This is a favorite verse for many believers but most of us quote only the first part, "I have been crucified with Christ and I no longer live, but Christ lives in me." As a young believer, I found it very difficult to live dead to sin and alive to God (Romans 6:11). "A dead man does not sin," I was told, so I would focus mostly on dying and asking Christ to live through me. That did not work very well because there was a problem with my thinking. I was not trying to live; I was trying to die. When the second part of that verse in Galatians came alive to me, I found the key to living the Christian life. The remainder of this verse in Galatians reads, "The life I live in the body, I live by faith in the Son of God, who loved me and gave Himself for me." It is not only Christ that must live in me; I must live also, but this life is in Him. The key is to know how to live both crucified and resurrected. We can do this by faith.

When Christ rose from the dead, we rose with Him (Ephesians 2:6). Many people see this as a positional truth, but I see it as real, but for only a part of my being. God's order for man is spirit, then soul, then body (1 Thessalonians 5:23). Salvation follows that order.

We have been saved in our spirit, we are being saved in our soul, and our body will be glorified at the resurrection. As we walk in obedience by faith, we obtain as a reward the salvation of our souls (1 Peter 1:9). We are newly created spirit beings, living in temporal bodies. When we walk with this understanding, we see that how we feel or think is not what is true, although it affects our behaviour. Our recreated spirit is quite willing to serve God, but our flesh is weak (Matthew 26:41). Having already obtained salvation for our spirits, we now take possession or our souls.

The second part of the verse in Galatians tells us that the life we now live, we live by faith "in" the Son of God. We have a new life in Christ. Our bodies have been assigned to death with Him on the cross, but our spirits have been raised with Him. We are in Him as members of His Body, each with a special function (Romans 12:4-5). Now Christ lives in us, not by displacing us but by helping us to live as a part of His spiritual body. His Spirit and our spirit live in unity in our physical bodies (1 Corinthians 6:17). Our souls are becoming spiritual as we choose to follow the Spirit while denying ourselves and bearing our cross. There is a conflict in our souls, but we overcome the sinful nature with the help of the Spirit (Romans 8:13). Sin continues to live in our bodies (Ro. 7:17), but it has no power over us because we have already died to this world (Romans 6:10-11). Our souls continue to be transformed by the renewing of our minds (Romans 12:2). This is a process. Through repentance and faith, with the Sword of the Spirit, we bring every thought captive to obey Christ (2 Corinthians 10:5). Sometimes our souls are not willing to obey, but God disciplines us in love. He is faithful and just and forgives our sins and cleanses us from all that is not right (1 John 1:9).

Understanding this conflict helps us to walk in victory by faith. As you celebrate the resurrection of our Lord, meditate on the victory that is yours in Him. Make this your prayer and confession:

Thank you, Lord, for my salvation. I have been baptized into the Body of Christ. I am a new creation. Because I died with You, I am no longer a slave to sin. I am crucified to this world, and I am alive to God in my spirit. When Christ rose from the dead, I rose with Him. You have caused me to be seated with Him in heavenly places. You have given Your Spirit to live inside of me. My spirit and Your Spirit live together in this body which is Your temple.

With my soul I set my mind on spiritual things; I choose to follow Your Spirit. I offer myself as a living sacrifice and submit my soul to be transformed by the renewing of the mind, that I may serve you acceptably (Romans 12:1,2). Search my heart and see if there is any offensive way in me and lead me in the everlasting way (Psalm 139:23-24).

The Women at the Cross: Courage to Care

BY MARNIE POHLMANN

Read **Matthew 27:45 – 28:10** watching for what the women in the story were doing.

Who were the women at the cross?

At the cross, what did these women witness?

What is the significance of these events?

What effect could these events have on the women who were there?

What memories of Jesus' words might they have remembered?

What kinds of fears and hopes do you think they had?

How would you have reacted if you had been there?

. . .

What did the women have in common with Joseph of Arimathea?

You are a woman at the cross where Jesus chose to die for you. What decision will you make? Will you live your daily life faithful to the Saviour who has risen and gives eternal life?

Discussion:

How did Jesus treat women, as opposed to how society treated them? What does this say about how God feels about women?

It took courage for the women to stay at the cross, and later to go to the tomb. How does it take courage today for you to live a life aligned with Jesus, faithful to Him, devoted to Him?

How were the women "rewarded" for their faithfulness to Jesus? How are we rewarded when we are faithful to God?

Suggested Study Answers

Who were the women at the cross?

- Mary Magdalene – Jesus had cast 7 demons from her
- Mary, mother of James & Joseph – 2 disciples named James, Joseph not a disciple but may have been a follower, James & Joseph's father was Alphaeous, so this Mary was probably his wife
- The mother of James & John, whose father was Zebeddee – both James & John were disciples – this woman was

concerned about her son's place in Jesus' kingdom. She did not understand the cost of following Jesus

Many women who had come from Galilee with Jesus:

- Followers,
- Women Jesus had healed,
- Women who supported Jesus,
- The Bible names some of these women in other places, like Joanna and Susanna, but does not name them here, so we are not sure which of them were or were not present at the cross
- Mary, mother of Jesus – we know this because other passages tell of Jesus speaking to her

These women were from all walks of life, occupations, lifestyles, and stages of life

At the cross, what did these women witness? What is the significance of these events?

- 3 hours of darkness – not an eclipse - God's displeasure
- Jesus crying out to God – separation from God (refers to God, not Father, as he usually did)
- Jesus' death – Jesus chose death – gave up his spirit
- Temple curtain being torn – symbolized the opening of mankind's access directly to God
- Earthquake – God's power and judgement – all the earth is affected by God (even the rocks cry out)

What effect could these events have on the women who were there? What memories of Jesus' words might they have remembered? What kinds of fears and hopes do you think they had? How would you have reacted if you had been there?

- Perhaps grief, confusion, fear, hope

- What others would you add?

What did the women have in common with Joseph of Arimathea?

- They did not flee, like the disciples.
- They stayed to care for Jesus' body.

Jesus was not popular at this point – he was considered a criminal, and any who were associated with him may be suspect. In that culture & society, women were "second-class" citizens, so they could have been even more vulnerable to persecution for aligning themselves with Jesus.

It took courage for the women to stay at the cross, and later to go to the tomb. How does it take courage today for you to live a life aligned with Jesus, faithful to Him, devoted to Him?

Count the cost but remember that our strength comes from God.

How were the women "rewarded" for their faithfulness to Jesus? How are we rewarded when we are faithful to God?

- He appeared to them first.
- We are rewarded by developing our personal relationship with Jesus – He values us greatly.

Message:

You are a woman at the cross, today. The cross where Jesus chose to die for you. What decision will you make? Will you live your daily life faithful to the Saviour who has risen and gives eternal life?

No matter what kind of woman you are,

- young or old
- married or single
- mother or businessperson
- hurting or healed,

Jesus values you and invites you to follow Him.

What circumstances are you in?

Maybe you feel like,

- in the middle of the day, your life is dark,
- the very foundations of your life shaking like an earthquake
- maybe you are grieving the death of a loved one
- maybe you are afraid that you will suffer somehow if you are seen with Jesus

No matter who you are, no matter what your circumstances are – you are welcomed through Jesus to walk with God every day.

Will you stand with Jesus, who chose to die for you on the cross?

Do you see that He has beaten death and offers eternal life – to you?

In your daily life, will you courageously and faithfully be associated with Jesus?

If you would like to know Jesus in a personal way, and walk with Him in your daily life, tell God right now. For more information about what walking with God looks like, speak to someone who already confesses to follow Jesus, find a church that celebrates Jesus' sacrifice of death for our sin, or write to the publisher of this book.

Do not put off deciding about what you will do, as a woman at the cross.

PART II
CREATIVE NON-FICTION

Photo by Sally Meadows

My Friend, My Saviour: Mary of Bethany

BY RUTH L. SNYDER

My name is Mary. You may know me as the sister of Lazarus and Martha.

I heard rumours about Jesus, the carpenter's son from Galilee—the challenging stories he told, how he stood up to the Pharisees, and how he healed people. But I didn't meet him in person until my brother invited him to our place for dinner.

I sat at Jesus' feet and listened. I wanted to find out who this Jesus really was. Martha didn't appreciate my choice. She thought I should help with the meal preparation. But that's another story.

After that first visit, Jesus visited many times. I loved to hear his stories. Jesus' love and patience amazed me. Jesus called me his friend!

One day Lazarus became sick. No matter what Martha and I did, his condition worsened. We sent an urgent message to Jesus, "Lord, the one you love is sick," (John 11:3). I thought he'd come right away. But he didn't.

Lazarus died.

I wept. For four long days.

Then Jesus came. And he wept.

I thought he was too late.

When we went to the tomb I cringed. By now my brother's body would be raising a big stink, literally. Instead, Jesus called Lazarus, and he came walking right out of that tomb. Jesus raised my brother from the dead. What power! Many of my Jewish friends and I understood he was the Messiah, the Promised One. I couldn't wait for the day he took the throne and put the Romans in their place.

Then, I heard more rumours. The Sanhedrin, a powerful group of religious leaders, was plotting to kill Jesus. How could this be? Didn't they understand who Jesus was?

Six days before Passover, Jesus came to visit. We honoured him with a dinner. I wanted everyone to know that Jesus was worthy of the highest honour, so I opened my precious bottle of nard perfume and poured it all over Jesus' feet. Then I wiped his feet. With my hair.

My actions outraged one of his disciples. Jesus told Judas to leave me alone. "It was intended that Mary should save this perfume for the day of my burial. You will always have the poor among you, but you will not always have me (John 12:7-8).

I pondered. What did Jesus mean? He would be King. Wouldn't he? Why was he talking about burial?

The next day, Lazarus, Martha, and I hiked to Jerusalem to celebrate the Passover. We were in the crowd that welcomed Jesus as he rode into Jerusalem on a donkey. Palm branches waving. Cloaks on the road. Shouting. Celebrating our King! It was happening. Finally! We would be free.

The disciples invited us to share their evening meal with them. After the meal was over, Jesus stood and washed our feet. Then he became troubled. He told us one disciple would betray him. He said he would only be with us a little while longer. Jesus shared many things I didn't understand.

What did this all mean? If he was our Messiah, why would he go away without becoming King?

The next day, I heard the chief priests and Pharisees had arrested Jesus. Some said the leaders paid people to give false testimony. Surely people would see through the scam?

I asked where Jesus was. Jerusalem was in an uproar. Finally, someone said Pilate was rendering a verdict. I shoved my way through the crowds. Running. Frantic for information.

"Here is your king." It was Pilate. He understood!

"Take him away! Take him away! Crucify him!" I gasped. What were these people thinking? Were they going to crucify their king? My friend? The Messiah?

The crowd parted. Soldiers came, dragging Jesus. I hardly recognized him. Thorns. Wounds. Blood. He struggled to walk under the weight of a rugged cross. My heart broke. This couldn't be happening.

I followed the crowd. Where were they taking him?

We trudged step by step to Golgotha. Pounding. Nails. Blood. I watched in horror. Soldiers crucified my friend between two criminals.

Jesus was innocent. Didn't the crowd understand Jesus was our king? It seemed like Pilate was the only one who got it right. He prepared a sign reading, "Jesus of Nazareth, the king of the Jews," which the soldiers fastened to the cross.

I wept. Jesus raised my brother. He was powerful. Why didn't he save himself? The tears wouldn't stop.

I heard Jesus say, "It is finished."

"With that, he bowed his head and gave up his spirit," (John 19:30).

Nothing made sense anymore. My hope died.

The first day of the week, Mary Magdalene invited me and some of her friends to go to the tomb early in the morning with spices. That was the least I could do to show respect for my friend.

We arrived at the tomb; it was open. Empty! We ran and told Simon Peter and the other disciples.

What could this mean? Where was his body?

Later that day, Mary Magdalene told me she had seen Jesus. He told her to tell us that he was returning to our God.

Could it be? Was he alive?

That evening, Lazarus, Martha, and I joined the disciples. We met in a room. Door locked. There were rumours. Soldiers said the disciples stole Jesus' body. We were afraid.

Suddenly, there was Jesus, standing among us. "Peace be with you!" (John 20:19-20).

He showed his hands and his feet. Then he instructed us to share his message with others.

It was really him. Jesus was alive!

I remembered what he taught us. He told us he was the Lamb of God. He said he came as the ultimate sacrifice for sins. My sins? Then I understood. I believed. Jesus forgave me.

He is more than my friend. He is my Saviour.

Carry the Cross

BY VALERIE RONALD

While traveling the dusty roads on the month-long journey from Cyrene, I occupied myself imagining the splendour of the Temple Mount rising from the center of my destination, the Holy City of Jerusalem. For years I had yearned to celebrate the Day of Passover at this epicentre of Judaism. Yesterday that lifelong dream was fulfilled when I joined the throng of pilgrims streaming through massive gates into the temple courts. Thrilled by the blast of silver trumpets echoing against the stone of the temple walls and the pulse of the ancient Hallel chanted by hundreds of Levite priests, I recall asking myself, *Simon, are you truly standing before the holy altar of Yahweh*? Then the snowy white lamb squirming in my arms brought home why I was there; to offer a perfect blood sacrifice, wholly acceptable to the Lord.

Today before dawn I rise to begin the return journey to Cyrene. I presume my sons, Alexander and Rufus, are somewhere in the traveling party as we pass out of Jerusalem's gates into the country. When I discover they are not, I retrace my steps back to the city to find them, concerned about their whereabouts.

Drawn by the roar of an excited mob, I step out from a narrow street into a scene of mayhem. I never expected to come upon such chaos here in Jerusalem, and on a Feast Day. Fists punching the air, voices yelling invectives, the crowd packs the open paved area in front of the Praetorium. I find myself absorbed in the seething throng, jostled and pushed until I am thrown against a rough stone wall near the open gate.

The object of the crowd's ridicule hardly seems worth their fury. Surrounded by a company of Roman soldiers, a man beaten and bloodied beyond recognition struggles under the burden of a heavy beam. I wince at the gruesome sight of the prisoner's back laid open by brutal flogging and his limbs purple and swollen from countless blows.

I have seen condemned prisoners before but none tortured so viciously. The man's face is a mass of open flesh where his beard has been plucked out; his brow gouged by the circlet of long, cruel thorns pressed on his head. Blood fills the hollows of his eyes, running down his chin to pool on the paving stones at his feet. Feeling the gorge rise in my throat, I am relieved I have not yet found my sons. They are too young to witness such a gruesome scene.

"Crucify him! Crucify him!" scream many in the mob, while soldiers goad the burdened prisoner forward through the gate. His clothing hangs in bloodied shreds, still I recognize remnants of the tasselled stole of a rabbi. Could this be the rabbi I have heard stories about ever since arriving in Jerusalem? The one rumoured to have healed the sick and raised the dead? Some even link the title Messiah to his name. Surely he does not deserve this inhumane treatment.

I want to shut out the awful procession; close my eyes to the pain and blood, my ears to the man's laboured gasps for air, my nose to the reek of sweat, but I cannot. The prisoner sags beneath the weight of the rough timber, stumbles then collapses to his knees at my feet. Sentenced to die, he is forced to carry the beam of his own cross to the place of crucifixion, but he can go no further.

Suddenly rough soldier hands grab me and shove me toward the man on the ground, shouting at me to pick up the beam and carry it. I feel the sharp prod of a Roman spear in my side and know I must obey or die. As I stoop close, the condemned man raises his head to look into my face. Roaring mob, forceful soldiers, the smell of blood fade before that capturing gaze. The pain and suffering creasing the man's brow and squinting his eyes cannot diminish the absolute love blazing out. I feel my heart suspend its beat for the length of that look, only to take it up again as a renewed heart, an alive heart touched by this almost-dead rabbi.

Hefting the rough wood across my shoulders, sticky blood stains my hands but I am not repulsed. Instead, strength courses through my limbs, enough to grip the beam with one hand and reach down the other to help the bleeding man to his feet. The crowd parts as we move toward Golgotha.

(based on Mark 15:21)

The End of a Pilgrimage

BY MARCIA LEE LAYCOCK

"As the soldiers led him away, they seized Simon from Cyrene, who was on his way in from the country, and put the cross on him and made him carry it behind Jesus" Luke 23: 26.

If I had taken another way, how different my life would have been. If I had turned aside when I heard the crowd, perhaps I would never have known about this man, let alone have been tethered to him in such an irrevocable way.

I tried to resist, tried to tell the Roman guards that I was on pilgrimage, here to celebrate the Passover in a place I had dreamed about since I was a child. My dreams sometimes were disturbing, but all my life I had felt drawn to this place, this time, this destiny.

They were not concerned about my reasons for being there. They had reasons of their own.

The cross beam was heavy, perhaps all the more because I knew what it was meant for. I'd seen the uprights on my way into the city, knew this man staggering in front of me would soon be pinioned on the two beams nailed together. Crucifixion, the cruelest of Rome's devices.

But it wasn't the weight of that wood that made me groan.

It was the look he gave me when he raised his head and looked at me, as they forced me to carry it. A look that seemed to say, this will be hard, but come, my son, do this for me and you will never be the same. I tell you truly, even if those Romans had not forced the beam onto my shoulders, I would have carried it for him. After just that one look. It felt more like a longed-for embrace. I would have carried that beam and let them nail me to it. I would have died in his place.

And I didn't even know his name.

It wasn't until we reached the place and they shoved me back into the crowd that I began to ask the questions that burned in my mind and heart. Who is this man? What has he done? Why do the crowds scream for his death?

The answers were spat from snarling lips. A rabble-rouser, a zealot, one who incited the people against Rome and caused all manner of harm to come to those who live in Palestine. The answer from the Jews was the one that tore at my heart: blasphemer. One who dared call himself God not only in the streets and on the mountain sides but in the very synagogues where true faith is taught.

But as he hung there, he looked at me again and I knew none of it was accurate. This man was no zealot, no rabble rouser. And if he called himself the son of God there could be only one reason—because it was true. I stared at him and could not comprehend how I knew these things. My pilgrimage had come to an end at the feet of a bloodied human being, a mere man, he seemed, who saw into my very soul and gave me everything I'd ever searched for, longed for from the depths of my being.

I watched him die and knew in those torturous hours he was giving me life.

Yes, if I had taken another way, how different my life would have been.

No Distance

BY GLORIA L. GUEST

Jerusalem was teaming with people on my first Passover in the Holy city. Although a solemn occasion it was also a jubilant one, since it commemorated the deliverance of our people and I felt caught up in the excitement and fervor, which many said was amplified by the presence of the man, Jesus of Nazareth, in the city.

I had only followed Jesus from afar, as part of the crowds that surged around him, wherever He went. There was an unknown quantity about Him that fascinated me. He was a simple carpenter's son but He spoke as one in authority! The talk amongst the people was that even the Scribes and Pharisees were in awe of His understanding of the Scriptures. I admit to enjoying watching their frustration in trying to trick Him into answering in ways that would condemn Him. But Jesus never fell for their sinister games and would turn it back on them. I respected Him for that. We the common people were always under the hawk-like eyes of the Pharisees and other religious leaders, just waiting to report us for the smallest of infractions. They had it coming!

I still did not really know what to think of this man called Rabbi by his own disciples and had not put my faith in Him. Besides, there were whisperings and rumours that it was becoming dangerous to associate with this man. Anytime I even thought of following him closer, the round, innocent eyes of my children and my wife Martha's trusting gaze came before me. *Too dangerous*! Yet I continued to follow him, from a distance.

And now I had found myself in Jerusalem with this same man. Everywhere He went during the week, crowds amassed around Him, always fringed by the muttering Pharisees, overseeing the scene like vultures ready for a choice piece of dead meat. Yet Jesus' popularity was evident and it held them at bay for fear of causing a riot, should they try to apprehend Him.

Until—there was a betrayal. By one of his own disciples! The news spread throughout the city like wildfire, from house to house, late into the night and early morning hours, with quick knocks on doors and furtive whispers in alleys. Jesus had been arrested! It turned into the longest day of my life as I followed the crowds to see what would happen. I kept my distance, of course, but I saw and heard so much; the shouts of the people, now stirred into a frenzy against Jesus, by the religious leaders who whispered from ear to ear that Jesus had claimed to be the Son of God, yelling, "Crucify Him! Crucify Him!" Was this what they really wanted? My confusion smothered my thoughts and I allowed myself to meld into the crowd as we moved to line the pathway to Golgotha. I saw Him pass by staggering under the load of his own cross, beaten beyond recognition. *Surely, this beaten, whipped man cannot be the Messiah!* Yet when He turned his bruised and bloody face towards a group of women who were weeping not far from where I stood, and then for a second turned His eyes on me, I felt my body go weak. *Did I not just see in His eyes and countenance the purest of love and compassion and something else—forgiveness?* My confusion grew. *Who is this man who could make me feel forgiven? Had I not brought my own Passover Lamb into the city to be a covering for my sins?* I fell into a stupor, almost as a drunk man, allowing myself to be pulled along, and a reluctant witness to the crucifixion of an innocent man. *Too ghastly to speak of!*

The gospel of Luke vividly describes His crucifixion and then what came next.

"It was now about noon, and darkness came over the whole land until three in the afternoon, for the sun stopped shining. And the curtain of the temple was torn in two. Jesus called out with a loud voice, "Father, into your hands I commit my spirit." When he had said this, he breathed his last. The Centurion, seeing what had happened, praised God and said, "Surely this was a righteous man." When all the people who had gathered to witness this sight saw what took place, they beat their breasts and went away. But all those who knew him, including the women who had followed him from Galilee, stood at a distance, watching these things (Luke 23:44-49)

The Centurion's words were eventually passed back to us. *Even the Centurion had felt something!* My heart, previously hardened to what I thought that I knew about this man, what I could understand, suddenly felt broken, humbled and—changed. *What had Jesus said one time? That, "I, when I am lifted up from the earth, will draw all men to myself?" (John 12:32)* I was stunned. *He's dead*!. Yet His words were as life within me. In that moment I felt more stirred to follow him, not from a distance, but as a true disciple, than I ever had before. *Yet how could I now?* Questions burned within me as I too beat my breast and mourned and wept. Still, I felt it—this wellspring of hope. I wondered about tomorrow and the next days to come. I knew even less than before. I was filled with grief that He was gone. But a glimmer of hope had befallen me from the shadow of His cross and as the ominous sky and rumbling earth chased me back down the way I had come, with each shaking step I took away from His cross—felt—*No distance!!*

The Innocent Man

BY VALERIE RONALD

I waited long at my dressing table for Zera to come braid my hair, but she did not appear. A light knock at my door did not come from her but another servant, someone I did not know.

"There has been an accident, my lady!", the flustered woman declared. "Young Zera has been trampled by a soldier's horse in the courtyard. She is gravely injured and may not survive. I will serve you now."

She bowed low but I swept her aside as I rushed out the door and down the wide marble staircase. Roman guards stood to attention for the governor's wife, but I paid them no mind. All I could think of was my sweet, loving Zera crushed by horse's hooves.

Since my husband, Pontius Pilate, became the governor of Judea, I had been lonely and unhappy in this foreign outpost so far from my native Rome. The primitive, rebellious city of Jerusalem seethed with unrest, always on the verge of breaking out in violence, therefore my movements were restricted for my own safety. The wives of some of Pontius' officials remained cool and aloof, so was it any wonder that my Hebrew maid servant, Zera, with whom I spent many hours, became my confidant? I noticed her bright eyes and quick, dimpled smile immediately, despite her deferential manner.

Gradually I drew her out, encouraging conversation, finding her to be warm and intelligent with a way of observing life that amused me.

Lately she had been full of stories about an unusual Jewish rabbi rumoured to perform miracles of healing the sick and raising the dead. Zera hadn't seen these miracles for herself but she had heard him teach near the temple. Her eyes glowed when she told me how he encouraged his listeners to love, forgive and seek the kingdom of God. Her words sparked in me a hidden desire to hear him for myself.

It is he whom I sought, desperately hoping he could help Zera, lying ashen and still next to me in my litter as it was carried hurriedly through the streets of Jerusalem. We came to a sudden stop on the edge of a dusty square where a man addressed a crowd of people pressing close to hear all he said. Dressed in simple rabbi's robes, he appeared ordinary enough yet he held the crowd spellbound with his words. This must be the one they called Jesus the Nazarene.

I bade my litter bearers to carry Zera's limp body to the man, going ahead to clear a way through the crowd. I did not realize I was crying until I fell to my knees before him, begging him to heal her. He listened, his warm eyes on my face infusing me with a strange peace.

"Do not weep, daughter of Rome. She will be restored to you."

Then he laid his hand on Zera's pale forehead. I watched her eyelids flutter open, her cheeks flush pink, and a small smile come to her lips when she saw the man who touched her. He gently raised her to her feet, placing her warm hand in mine. I could not speak for wonder.

I took Zera home in the litter, although she could have walked herself as she now appeared to be a picture of health. Those at the governor's palace who had witnessed the accident gaped at her when we returned. We did not discuss the miracle until we were alone in my chamber. Her torn and bloodied gown evidenced the reality of her injuries yet she had not a mark on her. We could only conclude that this Jesus had healed her. Questions and curiosity flooded our conversation. I wanted to know more about him but I must keep my inquiries hidden for the sake of this rabbi's safety.

Several nights later I woke with a cry, my heart leaping in my chest, my body damp with alarm. Early morning light stole through the draperies enclosing the bed where I struggled to escape the grip of a disturbing dream. I realized I was safe in my familiar bed chamber in the governor's palace, an armed guard standing watch outside the door. But the dregs of the vision would not leave, even when I rubbed my hands over my eyes, trying to dispel the image of a face filling my inner vision. The face of the Jewish rabbi.

Since Zera's accident I had found out little about the man who had healed her. My position as the wife of Pontius Pilate limited my access to those who could answer my questions. I had to tread carefully, yet I did ascertain that he was rumoured to be the Jew's Messiah, prophesied for centuries to be the saviour of their people. I also discovered that the Jewish ruling council viewed him as a threat.

I was surrounded by Roman officials who scoffed at the idea of a poor Jewish carpenter turned rabbi able to heal the sick and raise the dead, then dismissed him as delusional. Only in my dream he was no lowly peasant but a king in radiant robes, with stars in his hand and eyes like blazing fire. In the strange way of dreams, his robes slowly blossomed with spreading crimson stains and dark drops fell from wounds in his hands. The widening dreamscape revealed my husband crouching before him, wringing his hands over and over, trying to rid them of the blood of this innocent man, but the stains only grew darker. I knew this portentous dream had a purpose.

Pontius had told me late last evening of the rabbi's arrest by the Sanhedrin, the Jewish ruling council. If the rumours of their hatred of this man were correct, they would try to have him put to death. Under Roman law they were forbidden to carry out executions, which meant he would be handed over to Pontius, the governor. I tried to appear disinterested at this news, yet my hands had trembled within the folds of my gown.

Now by the pale light of dawn I froze with my fingers entangled in my hair. Surely Pontius would not order the execution of an innocent man? I knew him to be shrewd and fair-minded when it suited him, or he would not have been appointed governor of Judea. I also knew he could only remain governor as long as he delivered relative peace and stability in this occupied province. Which could mean he had no choice but to sentence the rabbi to death. Then blameless blood would be on his hands, just as in the dream, never to be cleansed.

Throwing on a robe, I called for parchment and ink and hastily penned a message to Pontius.

"Don't have anything to do with that innocent man, for I have suffered a great deal today in a dream because of him."

Pressing my signet ring into the sealing wax, I ordered a servant to deliver it at once to the governor. When Pontius saw it was from me, he would surely heed it. He must or I sensed the outcome would be ruinous. Throughout the morning I kept to my chamber, even banning Zera from my presence. Pacing the marble tiles, I stepped out onto the balcony only when I heard the roar of an angry crowd in the distance. Pontius did not reply to my message or come to me

At midday the sky suddenly darkened, plunging the land into an oppressive gloom. Black clouds roiled overhead yet brought no rain to relieve the heavy atmosphere. Through unnatural dusk I saw three execution crosses raised starkly upon the horizon atop the hill called Golgotha. Dread ran like ice in my blood. When an earthquake shook the floor beneath my feet, I took to my bed, staring wide-eyed into the shadows, afraid to dream.

But gradually sleep did come. And I did dream again, this time of a man mounted on a white horse, his robes dipped in blood. His face shone like the sun in all its brilliance and on his head were many crowns. On his robe and on his thigh was written: KING OF KINGS AND LORD OF LORDS. No fear tainted this dream. Instead a sense of profound peace filled me. He beckoned to me, holding out his hands in welcome. In the dream I went to Jesus the Nazarene, and knelt to touch the scars of crucifixion on his palms, now healed in an alive, glorified body.

(based on Matthew 27:19)

These Hands

BY SUSAN BARCLAY

His gaze met mine without a trace of rancour. And yet I held the power of life and death in my hands. The ability to order or deny his execution.

There was peace in his eyes, and my hands felt cold and sweaty. What to do with this man who seemed to hold no fear of death? Didn't he understand the cruel punishment of crucifixion? And it seemed to me, from the little I could get out of him, that he had done no wrong; that the Jews were afraid of him, despised him for some reason, perhaps envied him. They accused him of treason, but from all I could discern, he was no political threat to Rome, and if he were, the Jewish people would surely be on board if they thought he could overthrow us.

"Are you the king of the Jews?" I asked, clasping my hands at my waist.

"So you say," he replied.

I could see how he might aggravate, this enigma of a man. How he would rile the Pharisees, they who were all about law and order and giving the right answers. I decided to send him to Herod. Let him deal with him! The Jewish leaders weren't happy about it, but I wasn't happy about the position they were putting me in. It felt like entrapment; like no matter which course of action I took, I'd lose.

And then Herod sent Jesus back to me. Neither of us could find any fault in him. Then I remembered the practice of releasing a prisoner to the Jews at the Passover season and decided to let them choose between Jesus and Barabbas, a notorious and violent criminal. Surely they would choose Jesus, I thought.

My wife, Procula, hearing the chants and cries of the crowd, tried to intervene on Jesus' behalf and sent me a message. She'd had a nightmare involving him, and felt that no good could come of my participation.

Through it all, Jesus stood by, his hands at his sides, those peaceful eyes looking over the people, sometimes closing as if in prayer. I rubbed my wet palms on my robe as the crowd chanted for the release of Barabbas and the crucifixion of Jesus. I called for a basin of water, washed my hands ceremonially, and told them, "I am innocent of this man's blood. The responsibility is yours!" They called back, "We will take responsibility for his death - we and our children!"

I gave the order for Jesus to be flogged and to be turned over to the Roman soldiers for crucifixion. Then I took to my quarters and told my servants that I was not to be disturbed for any reason. But after Jesus died (so quickly I thought!), Joseph of Arimathea bulldozed his way in and asked permission to take Jesus' body and bury it in his own tomb. I granted it without even looking at him, and waved him away.

For three days I could not eat. I could not sleep. I avoided Procula - her comfort and companionship. I knew I couldn't look her in the eye.

And then I heard astonishing reports - that Joseph's tomb was empty, the stone had been rolled away and Jesus disappeared! More reports came: Jesus had been spotted alive, walking around, spending time with his disciples. How could it be? I wanted to see for myself, but was afraid and more than a little ashamed for my role in the killing of an innocent man. And if he *was* the King of the Jews, what might he do to me?

I look at my hands now and no matter how many times I wash them, they are never clean. His blood is on them. And for this I will be remembered.

I long for clean hands and a clean heart. I long for the peace that I saw in the eyes of Jesus.

I Know Him Not: Peter's Story

BY SANDRA SOMERS

I am the Apostle Peter, who greets you in the Name of Jesus. Grace and peace be multiplied to you. I'm here to tell you about the darkest night of my life so many years ago.

Jesus had been arrested. In the deep of the night, John and I watched in the distance as the mob bound Him and took Him to Caiaphas, the High Priest.

As I followed John and crept into the courtyard to watch events from a distance, the girl at the gate stared at me. I felt uncomfortable. "You're not one of Jesus' disciples, are you?" she asked.

"I am not," I said, a little too loudly.

I felt a coldness that was more than just the night air. To warm myself, I stood near the charcoal fire, its orange glow lighting up the courtyard.

A servant girl eyed me closely. "Didn't I see you with Jesus when they arrested him in the olive grove?" she asked. "Didn't I see you cut off my cousin Malchus' ear? You were with Jesus of Galilee. I know it," she said.

I rubbed my face as if trying to warm it up. But I knew I was trying to hide my involvement with Jesus. "I don't know what you're talking about!" I shouted.

Someone else chimed in. "Don't tell a lie. You're one of His followers. We can tell by your Galilean accent and your rough clothes. Why would a Galilean follow Jesus' arrest tonight if he weren't a Jesus follower?"

"I don't know the man!" I said. I swore, too. Ugly, vehement curses that echoed through the courtyard.

Just then the rooster crowed-once, twice. I caught sight of Jesus being led away, His hands tied behind His back. He looked deeply into my eyes and His words rang in my memory, "Peter, before the rooster crows twice in the early morning, you will deny Me three times."

Suddenly I remembered boasting hours before: "Even though others desert you, I never will."

What had I done! I crept to a hidden place and wept bitterly. There, wave after wave of memories rushed through me.

At Jesus' Transfiguration, I blurted out that we should make tabernacles—for Jesus, Moses and Elijah—before I even gave Jesus a chance to explain what was happening. Oh, my mouth was so quick to speak my impulsive ideas.

Then God's voice boomed out, "This is My Beloved Son. Listen to Him!"

I heard, but I didn't listen. Not then or later.

Once I even rebuked Jesus as if I were wiser than He. "You won't suffer and die!!" I didn't understand why He spoke so vehemently: "Get behind me, Satan!"

Then later, after our wonderful Passover dinner, Jesus took us to the Garden of Gethsemane where he walked a short distance away.

Even though I heard Him cry heart-wrenching sobs, I slept. I slept when He needed me the most. And then I ran away - deserted Him when He was arrested. I as much as thought, "Too bad for you! I need to save my own skin!"

Later that night, I denied even knowing Him—not once, not twice, but three times, just as He predicted!

As I wept bitter tears, I hated myself for my blustering and bravado and boasting. I wish I could have taken back all my words and my proud attitude. I had failed Jesus.

As I look back on those moments, my bitter tears became my first redemptive steps back to Jesus. But at the time I thought this was the end of my usefulness. I could never be what Jesus asked me to be - a fisher of men.

So, I went back to fishing.

After a miraculous catch of fish, we pulled to shore. And there was Jesus, ready to serve us breakfast over a charcoal fire. A charcoal fire! Memories and shame burned in me as I remembered those earlier embers.

"Simon, do you love Me?" He asked. He even used my old name. Not Peter the Rock, but Simon "the one who hears". Three times He asked if I loved Him. Three times! I was disturbed. Didn't He know I loved Him? Then I understood - one question for each time I had denied Him.

"Then feed my sheep… Feed my lambs," He said each time.

His forgiveness and grace washed over me. He was restoring me to a right relationship with Him.

But more. Jesus had seen my potential and was recommissioning me. From then on, the Holy Spirit filled me to go in His power to perform miracles in Jesus' name and to lead the growing church of Jesus' followers.

My One Special Job

BY SHARON ESPESETH

As an angel of the Lord, I had one special job coming up. I'd gone on previous assignments to earth, but this one was part of God's big plan of salvation. I felt honoured and excited, but nervous, to be chosen for this mission.

We, the angelic host, had been watching as God's plan began to take shape. During these past several weeks, anticipation and emotions ran high in heaven and on earth. Since Jesus' triumphant ride into Jerusalem on a donkey, the air around the Holy City became electric.

In heaven, we knew that God's sacrifice of His only begotten Son was His loving way to redeem His people from their sins. Jesus understood and agreed to God's plan. In spite of Satan's temptation to Jesus' human side, the Son surrendered to His Father's will. In the Garden of Gethsemane, Jesus prayed, "Father, if you are willing, take this cup from me; yet not my will, but yours be done (Luke 22:42)."

We watched from above that sorrowful Friday, as Jesus was tortured, taunted and hung on the cross to die. He, though innocent, bore the sins of the world.

From noon until about 3:00 p.m., the sky steadily darkened. About that time, Jesus cried out loudly in his own tongue, "My God, my God, why have you forsaken me (Matthew 27:45b)?" Some thought he was calling out for Elijah; others thought he was thirsty, so one of the guards brought him a sponge soaked with wine vinegar.

Jesus cried out loudly once more and He gave up His spirit. That's when the curtain of the temple was rent from top to bottom. As Matthew writes, "The earth shook, the rocks split, and the tombs broke open. The bodies of many holy people who had died were raised to life (Matthew 27:51b-52)." We saw all of this happen.

Everyone, including the guards watching Jesus, were stunned and terrified. They must have realized then that Jesus was more than an ordinary man. The people had been stirred with emotion, either in support of what had happened or broken-hearted by the way their beloved had been treated. Onlookers either loved and adored him or despised and rejected him.

Once the crucifixion was over, the crowds dwindled and dispersed across Jerusalem and into the country. To them, it seemed like everything was finished. In fact, that's what Jesus said right before He gave up his spirit on the cross: "It is finished (John 27:30)."

The sun was setting that Friday when the Jewish leaders went to Pilate and asked—maybe demanded—that the bodies of the three crucified men be removed from the crosses. They didn't want the bodies left on the crosses during the Sabbath. They also asked that the legs of the crucified be broken.

As commanded, the soldiers broke the legs of the thieves on either side of Jesus. Seeing that He was already dead, they didn't break His legs. Instead one of the soldiers pierced His side so that blood and water gushed out. The Roman soldiers were unaware that, by piercing Jesus' side rather than breaking His legs, they were fulfilling prophecy. See what John said in John 19:36-37.

The time had not yet come for me to do my part. I waited and watched like a percussion player waiting for the orchestra conductor to give the signal for me to play my one small part.

Meanwhile, Joseph of Arimathea, a rich man who had secretly become a disciple of Jesus, went to Pilate to ask for the body. By the time Joseph and his friend, Nicodemus, were in possession of the body, the sun had set that Friday night. It was the beginning of the Jewish Sabbath.

Since Joseph and Nicodemus were both of the Jewish tradition, they realized that by handling the body on the Sabbath, they'd be considered defiled. Nevertheless, the two of them carried Christ's body to the tomb Joseph had recently cut out of rock in a nearby garden. There they prepared His body for burial. They then rolled the huge stone across the entrance to the tomb.

Saturday, the Sabbath, was quiet. I still awaited my cue. Very early on Sunday morning, the chief priests and Pharisees went to Pilate with their concerns about the security of the tomb. "Sir," they said, "we remember that while he was still alive that deceiver said, 'After three days I will rise again (Matthew 27:63).'" The band of men asked Pilate to have the tomb safe-guarded until the third day, lest his disciples ". . . come and steal the body and tell the people that he has been raised from the dead" (Matthew 27:64).

Accordingly, Pilate ordered his soldiers to place the Roman seal on the heavy rock that barred entrance to the tomb. Anyone breaking this seal could be punished by an unpleasant death. The soldiers went immediately to do as commanded and to stand guard.

The time had come for my part in God's plan! As Matthew describes it in his gospel, "There was a violent earthquake, for an angel of the Lord came down from heaven and, going to the tomb, rolled back the stone and sat on it (Matthew 28:2)."

That was me!

Pilate's guards were unprepared for what had happened next. The stone rolled away and the tomb was empty except for Jesus' burial cloths. As I came out of the tomb in my bright angel attire, the soldiers looked like they were seeing a ghost. Forgive me, Dear God, for my laughter, but, as Matthew tells the story, "The guards were so afraid of him (me!) that they shook and became like dead men" Matthew 28:4.

That part of my work was done, so I just sat on the rock waiting for the next part of my mission.

Just after sunrise, a few women came to the door of the tomb with spices for anointing Jesus' body. On their way, they discussed the big stone. Who would roll it from the doors of the tomb?

I can still remember the expression on their faces when they saw the rock rolled away and me sitting on it. Flitting down from the rock, I began the speech I had prepared, "Do not be afraid, for I know you are looking for Jesus, who was crucified. He is not here; he has risen, just as he said" Matthew 28:5-6.

I may have said an Alleluia or two, because I was pretty excited. I invited them to see the place where the men had laid our Lord.

Then, as instructed, I said, ". . . Go quickly and tell his disciples: 'He has risen from the dead and is going ahead of you into Galilee. There you will see him" Matthew 28:7.

So that's how my special job played out. I'm humbled and happy to have had a small part in God's plan. There! Now, I've told you too. Alleluia! Jesus is risen. Alleluia!

Sharing a Son's Suffering

BY NINA FAYE MOREY

"Which of the two do you want me to release for you?" Pilate asked the raucous crowd.

A spark of hope filled my heart, but it was instantly snuffed out by the throng's wild shouts of, "Barabbas!"

"What shall I do, then, with Jesus who is called the Messiah?" Pilate demanded.

"Crucify him!" they shouted.

I gasped, clutching my breast. My heart felt as though it had been cruelly wrenched from my chest. I'd always known this day was coming, but I'd buried that knowledge in the dark recesses of my mind. Now there was no escape. Tears brimmed in my eyes, blurring my vision.

"Why? What crime has he committed?" Pilate responded, trying to restore some reason to this unruly mob. Pilate was no fool. He knew why the chief priests and elders had brought Jesus before him. They'd whipped up the masses into this frenzied state, convincing them to demand Jesus's crucifixion.

The seething horde simply shouted even louder. "Crucify him!"

Blinded by my tears, I tried desperately to force my way through the crush of the crowd. If only I could reach my precious son. Tears streamed down my cheeks, but I made no effort to wipe them away. I needed to get to Jesus, to wrap my arms around Him and protect Him, as I'd always done.

Pilate now realized there was no hope of reasoning with this rabble. Amidst the roar of the crowd, he rose from his judge's seat and poured water over his hands, symbolically washing away any culpability for what was to come. "I am innocent of this man's blood. It is your responsibility!"

Afterwards, Pilate released Barabbas and ordered Jesus flogged before handing Him over to be crucified. My hands flew to my mouth to stifle my anguished cries. Then, as the governor's guards scourged my son's flesh, I heard a scream… my own.

I followed the Roman soldiers as they led Jesus to the governor's palace. There they stripped my son of His clothes, dressed Him in a scarlet robe, and fashioned a crown of thorns which they placed upon His head. I wrung my hands helplessly as blood began trickling down His forehead. Then the soldiers put a staff in Jesus's right hand and knelt before Him, mocking Him with, "Hail, King of the Jews!" They spat on Him, took the staff, and began striking His head repeatedly. My heart ached to cup my son's disfigured face in my hands, kiss His swollen lips, and tell Him once more how dearly I loved Him.

Finally, the soldiers put Jesus's clothes back on Him. Then they forced Him to carry His own cross as they led Him away to be crucified. Weak from the flogging, Jesus collapsed and was unable to continue up the hill to Calvary. My heart broke at the sight of my once strong carpenter son brought to His knees by the weight of that heavy timber. The soldiers pulled a man from the crowd, Simon of Cyrene, forcing him to carry Jesus's cross. When they reached Golgotha, "the place of the skulls," they began nailing my son's hands to the cross.

Every time a soldier pounded a nail through Jesus's hands and feet, I felt as though it were piercing my heart. Those hands I'd held so tightly; those feet I'd washed so tenderly. When the soldiers hoisted that heavy cross and let it fall into its moorings, sobs suddenly wracked my body. I huddled close to the foot of the cross; determined to keep vigil over my dying son despite the vitriol flung by belligerent bystanders.

I remained by my son's side throughout the growing darkness; silently pleading with God to quickly end His suffering. How much more could Jesus endure? At last, I heard Him cry out, "It is finished." No more pain; no more suffering. "Thank you, God!" Despite my deep sorrow at the loss of my precious son, I finally felt at peace, knowing He was now in the loving hands of His Heavenly Father.

Today

BY WENDY L. MACDONALD

Today.

Today, I die.

I don't understand why they're crucifying Jesus too.

Blood oozed from every wound and pore of Christ's body. Flies as numerous as those I felt on my own pierced hands and feet feasted on the fluids that dripped as He drifted closer to death.

Pain, nausea, and putrid odors staved off any hunger and thirst I may have otherwise suffered as well.

Are the religious leaders jealous because Jesus has already grown a large following? Did they think He would have robbed their pockets of what they've already picked from other people?

I am a thief but Jesus is no criminal.

The only things He seems to have stolen are the hearts of the ordinary people through the good deeds He has done.

But why doesn't He save Himself?

He saved the blind, saved the sick, and raised the dead. What benefit is it for a good man to die and leave bad men to carry on with their corruption?

Is there something I'm not understanding?

"Stop," I tried to shout, but only rasped, as the other thief who's as guilty as me mocked Christ.

Why does he join the haters?

Doesn't he know the miracles this man of God has done? And yet, I haven't heard a word of Jesus asking payment for the healings. No begging from a man who begs our respect. He owns nothing of this world, and yet, I sense He has the power to rise up, dethrone, and take the crown Himself.

I suck in my breath and attempt to shout, but only a hoarse whisper sounds. "Stop, he hasn't sinned. We deserve this cruel death. But not He who has been good and kind - even perfect."

Jesus turned His head and looked at me, eyes brimming with compassion.

I turned away, ashamed.

How does He have anything left to share?

Doesn't He see my lifetime of thievery - my lifetime of caring little for others and caring lots for booze, bread and the beds of wayward women?

Oh, God, I have sinned to the depths of darkest hell. I deserve this torture.

I returned my gaze to His battered body. A tear, a single tear, slipped down the torn, holy, and swollen cheek that faced me.

Does He weep for me?

For all who have rejected God? Is it too late to turn away from all I've been and done? Oh, wretched thief that I am. How could I think to ask for mercy when I lived mercilessly?

He nodded. A single nod is what Jesus gave me.

Has He read my mind?

Did He see all of it? So much sin abides in me. I crave to die free from the memory and the stench of it all, a stench worse than the filth of these stained crosses. Can He do this? Is He truly the Son of God as He claimed to be?

I saw love. I saw mercy. I saw… God… in Him.

Yes, He is God in the flesh.

"Jesus," I heard myself say, "Will you remember me when you go to be with the Father?"

Before He replied, a flood of power whooshed through my body and soul. I felt clean. I was forgiven. I felt a peace, joy, and love I've never known.

Jesus, the Messiah, answered me, and I know He spoke the truth when He promised I would be with Him in His Father's kingdom.

Today.

Today I live.

Jesus answered him, "Truly I tell you, today you will be with me in paradise."

Luke 23:43 NIV

The Passion Through John's Eyes

BY LYNN DOVE

John looked out at the crowds of shouting people who had gathered along both sides of the road. Jerusalem was more crowded than usual at this time of year, with people amassed to celebrate the Passover. He was hidden in a doorway, shading his face in the folds of his prayer shawl. There in the shadows he kept silent watch as the Roman procession came closer into view. The last twenty-four hours had been spent following his beloved friend from trial to trial, always watching from a safe vantage point. Fear overwhelmed him, not only for himself, but for his friend.

He had been there the night they arrested Jesus. He had been aroused forcefully from a dreamless sleep, initially uncertain what the noise and commotion around him was all about. Now fully awake and under the glow of torchlights, he saw Judas kiss Jesus on the cheek in greeting and then step aside to allow a Roman guard to grab hold of Jesus' arm. Before John could react, another of his closest friends intervened by pulling out the knife he always carried to cut fishing line and netting, and cut the ear off of the guard trying to arrest Jesus. John recoiled in horror just remembering the blood and the brutality of the act that night. It had happened so quickly! In the aftermath, he had fixed his eyes angrily on Judas, furious by his betrayal of Jesus. Judas had jumped back just in time to avoid the knife attack. *It would have served him right*, he thought, and instantly regretted thinking it. "Forgive me, Lord," John silently prayed as he now huddled in the shadows on the crowded street. "You warned us this would happen. I didn't understand. Even when you touched the guard and healed his ear, you showed compassion, when all I thought about was revenge. Forgive me."

As sweat beaded on his forehead, he peeked out just far enough to see the Roman soldiers, some on horseback, several others following behind on foot, whipping and cursing the three prisoners in their charge. John took note of two of the men, thieves he surmised, by the derogatory taunting and stone-throwing aimed at the two. A small wagon, pulled by a donkey, carried the cross braces while the men walked dejectedly beside the wagon and ducked and railed against the crowd with uncommon bravado in the face of their inevitable death sentence. Following much more slowly behind them, John saw his friend.

Jesus was almost unrecognizable. They had beaten, scourged and brutalized him with unimaginable cruelty. Tattered, flayed skin, criss-crossed his slender frame, revealing muscle and tendon. Blood oozed and ran down his body in rivulets. The crowd suddenly grew silent, revolted by the misery and anguish they now saw in human form in front of them. The soldiers had spared him no quarter. Unlike the two men ahead, his heavy cross was not in the back of the donkey-pulled wagon. He dragged his cross upon his own shoulders despite the horrible wounds that the praetorian guards had inflicted on him.

He stumbled and dropped to his knees right in front of where John was hiding. John winced in empathy as a crown of thorns cut jagged grooves into Jesus' temple. The crown, along with the seamless purple robe they had draped over him, had been yet another cruel attempt by his captors to mock the claim of Jesus being a "king". The guards, now impatient with this delay, lashed him with leather whips. Some in the crowd, horrified by this, were now shouting, "Mercy! Have mercy on him!" Ignoring the yells, the guards continued their assault. With super human effort, Jesus adjusted the cross on his back and slowly rose to his full height, but could not seem to make his feet move forward. John, without thought now for his own safety, moved from his hiding place towards his friend to help him, but was held back by a soft tug on his robe from behind. Turning, he saw her face.

Mary, Jesus' mother, pleaded with her eyes for John not to interfere. She held out her hands to him and with great compassion, John enfolded her in a soft embrace. She clung to him, his arms tightly wrapped around her slender form, and then she collapsed onto him weak-kneed and weeping with despair. John cradled her face to his chest, but she forced herself to look past him towards her son, who trudged past them now with grim determination. When Jesus stumbled and fell again, the cross landing heavily on top of him this time, John felt Mary's body jolt forward but he wouldn't release his grip on her.

Exasperated now, one of the guards caught sight of a giant of a man and pulled him forcibly out from the crowd and ordered him to carry the cross for Jesus the rest of the way up the hill to Golgotha. John, hugging Mary to his side, followed the sombre procession with the rest of the crowd, as they slowly made their way up the hill.

The sound of metal striking bone and wood resonated as the guards drove the long spikes through the wrists and feet of the prisoners, securing their bodies to the crosses. John was numb, watching the crosses being raised, one on each side with Jesus in the middle. He watched in disgust as the guards took Jesus' clothes and divided them into four shares, one for each of them, and cast lots for the seamless robe. John remembered one of David's psalms, "They divided my clothes among them and cast lots for my garment." Scripture was being fulfilled right in front of him!

The crowd dispersed quickly once the gruesome spectacle of the execution sentences had been carried out. From previous experience, most people soon got bored of how long it took for prisoners to die on a cross. It was not long before John realized that he and Mary were amongst only a handful of others who remained at the foot of the cross. He glanced around and saw Jesus' aunt, Mary the wife of Clopas, and Mary Magdalene, all weeping mournfully together, with their eyes upturned towards the face of Jesus. John raised his own eyes and re-read the sign that was nailed to Jesus's cross. Written in Aramaic, Latin and Greek, all three languages familiar to John, he remembered the heated exchange only hours before between Pilate, the Roman Governor, and the chief priests during Jesus' trial. Pilate had finally succumbed to public pressure to execute Jesus, but as a parting shot at the Jewish leadership, had been adamant that a sign be nailed to the cross saying, 'The King of the Jews'. The Jewish leaders had complained vehemently about the wording, but Pilate answered, "What I have written, I have written."

John gazed up into his friend's face and Jesus looked directly at him. John shuddered involuntarily. Even in his dismal state, Jesus was still fully aware of his surroundings and of those who had gathered around him. Jesus painfully raised his head up so he could speak boldly. "Woman," he called to his mother, "here is your son." His eyes looked from Mary to John and then leveling a piercing gaze upon John said, "Here is your mother." The intent was clear. John was now fully responsible for Jesus' mother, Mary. As she leaned into him, he lightly put his arm around her shoulder. John nodded to indicate he would willingly carry out this last request for his friend. Mary would always have an honoured place in his home.

John barely noticed the passage of time there on the hill. Jesus conversed with the two men hanging on their crosses beside him, but John did not take note of the words they exchanged. The hours passed. There was little movement now from the three men. John leaned forward to hear laboured breathing from one of the thieves, and then was startled when Jesus suddenly cried out, "My God, my

God, why have you forsaken me?" Someone murmured, "God has turned his back on him." John knew better. Jesus was quoting that same psalm of David that had been brought to John's mind when the guards were casting lots for Jesus' clothing. Weak from his torture on the cross, Jesus only had the strength to speak the first line but John had memorized the entire psalm too. He had sung it as a child in synagogue. It was so familiar to him and yet he never quite understood what the words meant until that very moment. He softly whispered the last line, "They will proclaim his righteousness, declaring to a people yet unborn: He has done it!"

Finally, as the afternoon wore on, Jesus muttered, "I am thirsty." A Roman guard soaked a sponge on a stalk of hyssop plant with wine vinegar and lifted it to Jesus' lips. When he had received the drink, John saw Jesus lift his eyes to the heavens. It was as if he knew what awaited him now. Everything had now been accomplished so that Scripture was fulfilled, and Jesus called out triumphantly, "It is finished." With that, Jesus bowed his head and gave up his spirit.

John took hold of Mary then, clutching her to himself as they wept together in mutual anguish. The sky grew ominously dark and the earth trembled. They held each other, oblivious to the world around them. Still grief stricken, John reluctantly let go of her. Mary, unhindered now, boldly approached the cross and reached up to touch the calloused feet of her beloved son. John followed and warily laid his fingers upon the blood encrusted toes of his dear friend. With an impact he had never felt before, John felt a jolt course through his entire body. The sensation nearly brought him to his knees. Unmistakable, distinctive words formulated themselves in his mind, so clearly in fact, he thought he could hear Jesus' voice speak them! He didn't understand their meaning at first, but he somehow knew that their explanation and intent would be revealed to him in time. John gazed up into the peaceful face of Jesus, and the words continued to manifest themselves in his heart and mind. He would never forget them.

"In the beginning was the Word, and the Word was with God, and the Word was God. He was with God in the beginning. Through him all things were made; without him nothing was made that has been made. In him was life, and that life was the light of all mankind."

(This narrative is based on the Biblical text from the Gospel of John 19:1-30; Psalm 22, and John 1:1-4).

Hell: How I Got Here—Judas's Story

BRUCE ATCHISON

If only I had listened to the Christ! If only I had understood the opportunity I had. But I didn't and here I am in this horrid place. What a FOOL I was!

When Jesus of Nazareth came to Jerusalem, I knew I must join him. This Galilean was more than a mere rabble rouser. There was something different about him and his "Kingdom of Heaven" speeches. I felt he would really be our Messiah, the one to kick out the oppressive Romans and make Israel great again.

And unlike Theudas and other rebels, this Jesus did mighty miracles. I saw with my own eyes how the blind were given sight instantly. There was none of that fakery like the phony healers and the quacks practice. People actually were healed of incurable illnesses like leprosy. He even raised people who were stone-cold dead.

Then this rabbi sent us out, two by two, to proclaim his Kingdom. I didn't really know what it was all about but I repeated the words of the master like I was told to do.

I also was able to cast out demons like my partner and the other disciples. When we returned and told Jesus that even the demons obeyed us, he said our names were written in heaven. I thought he'd congratulate us but he just gave us a platitude. Was that all we could expect from the one who could have liberated Israel?

Then Jesus slipped into a funk. He kept saying he was going to Jerusalem to suffer and die. How could that be? He was our only hope to kick those foreigners out of our land and free us from their pagan ways forever! I started asking myself why I was hanging around this contradictory leader.

Then, as some might say, the last straw happened. Jesus let an immoral woman pour expensive perfume all over his feet. That alabaster box of spikenard could have been sold for a year's wages. I said it should have been given to the poor but I wanted my share of all that money. After all, I had the cash bag and none of those empty-headed followers suspected that I took what I wanted from it. I had to live too, you know.

That's when the Devil himself entered me. I really didn't feel like myself as I went to the Pharisees and cut a deal. It was like being in a bad dream. I supposed I could have gotten more money for showing them where the Christ would be alone. But a deal is a deal and I wanted nothing more from my former master.

Well, you know the rest. Jesus was arrested and tried. The whole time, he made no protest. I began to have second thoughts as the crowds insisted that Pilate crucify him.

Satan left me after I betrayed the Lord and my conscience tortured me. I took the money back to the Pharisees but they wouldn't take it. So, I threw it into the temple and left.

My conscience screamed at me as I walked the streets. The only way I knew to rid myself of that guilt was to hang myself. I found a tree with a limb growing over a cliff and made a noose of my tunic.

Suddenly, my guts fell out and I was in extreme agony. It felt much worse than my nagging conscience.

But that pain was nothing compared to the agony I now am in. No words can express the utter despair I feel and the relentless shrieking of my conscience. I knew the gospel and had been with the Son of God and yet I threw it all away for thirty pieces of silver. What an idiot I was!

Obsession with a Tomb

BY BOB JONES

My dear wife was completely perplexed by my obsession with the tomb.

Our garden was an oasis of sanctity and cessation from a city that feeds on frenzied pilgrims. We traded the noise and dirty streets for flowers, butterflies, gravel pathways, and stone steps. Many a late afternoon Seudah Shlishit on Shabbat had been eaten under the shelter of our olive tree.

Where my obsession came from I didn't know. But carving out a tomb in the rock face of our garden long before it would be needed was my passion. My preoccupation confused and irked my wife no end. And to be honest, the urgency to finish also confounded me.

But now I knew why.

Pharisees

Growing up in one of Jerusalem's wealthiest families, I lacked nothing. When I was seventeen years old, I felt Jehovah's hand on my life to search and gain insight into the laws and customs of the three sects of our nation - the Pharisees, Sadducees, and the Essenes. I adhered to the former – "one who is separated" - addicting myself to great austerities. Learning of Malachi, a holy man, who dwelt in the desert, and lived an austere life, I went and sat at his feet, and imitated his course of life for four years.

Returning to Jerusalem I met and married my wife, settling into life as a Pharisee, and became a member of the Sanhedrin. We received the backing and goodwill of the common people, in contrast to those aristocratic monarchists, the Sadducees. We were eclectic and more democratic. I might even say, popular. We preserved the oral tradition of the Talmud against the ridiculous literal interpretation of the Sadducees, even though they were among the high priests.

Rabbi Jesus

When Jesus of Nazareth began to take upon him the great work of public teaching, I was enamoured with his holy life, pure doctrine, and supernatural miracles. Many Jews embraced what he taught them, and I too became a great admirer of his preaching. I became a sincere convert and followed Rabbi Jesus in all the journeys he took throughout the land of Judea, and Galilee. At first, my association was without concern.

When Jesus ran afoul of the Sadducees I aligned myself even stronger with him. But when my brothers took offense at his declension of certain Levitical ritual laws, my standing was put at risk. As a respected member of the Sanhedrin it would not be taken lightly to be seen consorting with him. And so, I followed from afar.

The late night summons aroused me from a deep sleep. The Council was meeting. Some urgent judicial decision needed to be rendered. Arriving at the gathering I was shocked to see Jesus, under arrest, chained and bleeding. "Blasphemy." The charge was unfounded and the witnesses unreliable. But my brothers were devoted to seeing him guilty. I was silent. I could not consent to their decision and action. They led him away.

The Decision

The next day was agony. The Romans scourged Jesus, and now the crowds had turned against him and called for him to be crucified. Chaos reigned. The city had gone mad. At three in the afternoon the sky went black, and an earthquake shook Jerusalem. The world was surely coming to an end. Golgotha was frenzied. With Sabbath approaching, the Roman soldiers broke the legs of the criminals to expedite their deaths. Jesus was already dead – the blood and water from his pierced side was evidence of his broken heart. The sun was setting.

"Why would you, a Pharisee, want the body of a blasphemer?" My petition to Pilate brought some confusion with the authorities and consternation from my peers. The time for secrecy was over. And now my obsession with a tomb made sense. The linen shroud, the burial spices, a quick anointing and an unexpected helper – Nicodemus – another Pharisee, and silent follower. How many more were there?

We rolled the stone across the face of the now occupied tomb. The sun disappeared. The garden was silent.

My heart was as cold as the stone.

Joseph of Arimathea's Monologue

BY CAROL HARRISON

Well-dressed, educated, confident rich man which shows in his tone of voice. Months after Jesus' death, burial and resurrection, Joseph returns to the empty tomb and reminisces about that day he asked for the body of Jesus.

I bought this tomb a long time ago. I wanted to be prepared and used my considerable wealth to purchase this, my final resting place. I thought it appropriate for someone of my status to rest in this garden. When I died no one needed to worry about where to place my spice laden, linen wrapped body. It's empty now but no longer brand new. I used it once for my friend, Jesus. Let me share this amazing story with you.

My name is Joseph from Arimathea. I am a prominent member of the council—yes, the same council that plotted to do away with Jesus. They insisted he needed to be stopped because his message was against God. They accused him of blaspheme but I couldn't agree with them, not once I became well acquainted with the one they called Jesus.

You may think me a coward since I quietly became his disciple. I followed his teachings and believed with all my heart he was the Messiah the prophets had foretold. We had waited for God to send him and now he was here and those around me, who knew the Holy Scriptures, chose to plot his destruction rather than believe. I believed but I didn't dare make my beliefs public if I wanted to influence the council.

But the council wouldn't listen to reason. They hated him—maybe for showing up their faults—maybe for revealing all their man-made rules—or maybe because He never bowed to them and called them vipers and unclean which really angered them. Whatever the reason, they didn't accept him like I did.

I strongly opposed their decision to arrest Jesus, falsely accuse him, and get Pilate to let them crucify him. Their actions were not my actions but I couldn't stop them.

The Romans knew how to inflict suffering on those they hung on the cross. It was a slow, agonizing death. Men begged for mercy and something to dull their hours and hours of pain as life ebbed away. Yet Jesus begged God to forgive those who nailed him on to it and then he gave his life with one final cry, "It is finished." The centurion speared Jesus in the side and watched the blood and water flow out. I heard the Roman centurion who proclaimed him dead mutter how this must have been the Son of God.

I couldn't leave his body hanging on that cross over the Sabbath. I hadn't been able to stop the crucifixion, set in place by the council, but now it was within my power and ability to do one last thing for Jesus.

(*Joseph's tone becomes bold*)

I went to Pilate and asked permission to bury Jesus so our Jewish Sabbath rules would not be violated by a body hanging in public. He gave it with no problem. I bought fine linen cloth, only the best for my Lord and wrapped Jesus' body before laying it in this new tomb I had cut out of the rock, intended for my own use. I rolled a stone in front of the opening. It became a fitting burial place for Jesus. The Romans soldiers sealed the entrance and stood guard.

Then I left to mourn and observe the Sabbath.

(*his tone becomes full of wonder and joy*)

On the third day, the most amazing thing happened. When some of the women, who followed Jesus, went to the garden to anoint his body, they found the stone had been rolled away. The tomb was empty—just like you see it today. I stare into this tomb. I know exactly how I placed the body of Jesus. The linen cloths are here but Jesus is gone. My tomb is empty again—only borrowed for a short time.

He's alive! Jesus is alive. He rose from the dead just like he said he would. I didn't understand before but I do now. Jesus, the Son of God, who conquered sin and death loved us enough to take our punishment for sin. I will gladly follow him for the rest of my life, whether the council believes He was our long-awaited Messiah or not. Will you join me in following Him?

I Saw Him Dead

BY ALAN ANDERSON

"Now the centurion, and they that were with him watching Jesus, when they saw the earthquake, and the things that were done, feared exceedingly, saying, 'Truly this was the Son of God.'" Matt. 27: 54 English Revised Version.

Please allow me to discuss with you a few of my thoughts about Christ's crucifixion. I must ask you to not mention this to any other soldiers. They would not be pleased with me.

I've been a Roman soldier for a number of years - more than I can remember. As a Centurion, I have men I am responsible for and who automatically obey my commands. These men know better than to disobey me.

There are parts of my work I do not like. I hate crucifixions the most. I've seen men and women being crucified. I have witnessed them lingering before they died. Crucifixion is a brutal way to die. Roman law deems it for some people, therefore we carry it out. My men would rather crucify someone than disobey Roman commands. They would suffer themselves at the hands of the state if they disobeyed.

I have to say the crucifixion that bothered me most was that of Jesus Christ. I was there when this man was arrested, but before that I even saw Him heal someone. At the time we arrested Jesus, one of the men with Him sliced off the ear of one of my men with his sword. Just as I pulled my sword out of its sheath, Jesus stepped forward. He placed his hand over the man's bloody ear and healed it. Now, that I will never forget!

Jewish priests and members of the Sanhedrin made a huge fuss over Jesus when He was brought to trial. They acted as if He was the vilest criminal they had ever laid eyes on. They wouldn't shut up until they had a chance to make their terms known. They were determined to have Jesus punished.

My men and I agreed Jesus didn't seem threatening at all to us. He didn't scream or yell back when charges were made against Him. He just stood there, kind of like a sheep waiting to be slaughtered.

As you know, Jesus was sentenced to death by crucifixion. People even cried out to have Him executed. I didn't know religious people could be so cold and heartless until those Jewish leaders witnessed His punishment. Some even had smiles on their faces.

I remember His face most of all. As He hung on His cross Jesus looked right at me. It felt like He could see into my soul. I wanted to look away from Him but I just couldn't.

Jesus died. I was there when a few of His friends took His body down from the cross. I saw Him dead.

I also witnessed something else. That one morning, after His burial, it was discovered that His body was missing. There is no way His body had been stolen. He had come back from the dead. I couldn't believe it at first but there was no other explanation.

To have a man so brutalized, betrayed and killed, come back from the dead, staggers my mind and changed my life. For something like this to happen shook my conscience just like the earthquake shook my world. I realize now I have been a walking dead man.

Through His resurrection, Jesus paved the way for my resurrected life as well. He truly is the Son of God! He has given me a peace I've never known. This peace is strange to me, yet it is real.

There is an urge within me to inform other people that Jesus came back to life. Perhaps I'll find opportunities to tell my soldiers and officer colleagues about what I witnessed. He has risen! Indeed, He is risen!

The Point in the Story

BY MARNIE POHLMANN

It was still pre-dawn when my companions and I were called to duty. This was my first time. I was excitedly concerned about what I would be tasked with. I was confident, though, that whatever it was I would do it well. I had been held to the flame and hammered into shape. I was strong, big, and fit for duty. I was made for this day.

We were gathered at the top of a hill. The older ones among us called this hill "Golgotha" which meant "Place of the Skull" and I wondered why. It felt like a place of death, though, where spirits battled over souls. I looked at the ground on which I waited. Was that a bone fragment? Was this dirt darker than the dirt of my birthplace? Perhaps stained with blood? What did this mean for me? Why was I here?

The whispered comments and complaints of other junior consorts soon stilled as we waited. Some of the older ones had been in service here before, so if they were now satisfied to wait for action, then I would lay quiet, content as well.

We did not wait long. Soon a quiet rumble of voices became shouting and cursing that filled the air. The ground trembled with crowds pushing and shoving their way to the hilltop. A centurion gained control of the situation with authoritative commands and the crowd parted.

I was shocked by what I saw. A man stumbled forward, a wooden beam over his back. Blood dripped over his face from thorns that had been cruelly pushed into his brow. I wondered how the man was even standing, he looked so weak. Ah, I saw… on the other side was a strong, dark-haired man helping him bear the load.

"Close enough," barked the Centurion.

I watched the helper lay down the rough beam and rush away into the crowd like he wanted nothing more to do with the situation. I could see why. Left with the complete weight of the wood, the blood-covered man stumbled and fell. I could see his back as he lay there; or rather what should have been his back but was only tattered bits of skin clinging to raw meat. Was he already dead? He had obviously been severely whipped.

From the crowd, soldiers led two other men. These men fought every step, pulling against the ropes that bound their hands, only to be yanked forward by the guard or pushed forward by the crowd.

Soldiers were ordered to push the wood closer to the hole it would stand in. Two other holes already had crossbeams beside them. The soldiers then laid the captives on top of the wood.

I suddenly realized what I was going to be part of. No! This is not what I dreamed of doing with my strength. This was degrading, disgusting work. A crucifixion of criminals was the lowest job I could have been given. Had I done something wrong? Was I not one of the best?

I stayed back behind others as some of the old and new with me were grabbed and taken to the wood. Screams and pleas of mercy filled the air, causing me to tremble in fright. I could see the feet of one thief held tightly as the commissioned spikes were ordered in. The thief was in excruciating pain and twisted his upper body trying to hit anyone nearby. Then his arms were caught and held tight as the rope was removed from his wrists. His head was forced back, so he lay on the beam and his arms were forced out from his body, stretching along the crossbeam. As the nails were pounded through his palms his screams became whimpers. There was no longer any hope for him.

The cross was lifted by a group of strong soldiers, the bottom falling into the hole with a heavy thud, jarring another scream of pain from the thief on the cross. Quickly the soldiers braced the cross in place and hurried away, their job done.

So intent was I in watching this horror I did not see the soldier come to grab me from among those of us left in the pile. I tried to slip out of his grasp, but he gained a strong hold on me. One of my mates began a tinny, high-pitched wail as he clung to other nails. I prayed I would be strong in fulfilling my duty, no matter how distasteful it became.

And then I was given my task for the day. I was directed to secure the man's right hand. Odd, I thought, as I was led to my post at the center cross. This was the man wearing the crown of thorns, yet he was not screaming. I could see he was conscious, aware of what was happening. I looked into his eyes and saw the pain, yet there was also compassion as he looked at me. I reached for his hand and it was as though he reached toward me, offering to be held by me. I shook and wished I could pull away, but he nodded ever so slightly like he was reassuring me that this was my duty and I needed to do it well.

I turned to stare at his hand and pressed my chiselled point into his weathered palm. Then the hammer fell. It struck my head, driving my newly forged body through the man's flesh, sinking my point deeper and deeper through the hand with each blow and continuing until I was buried deep into the wood behind it. My head was exploding with pain and could not grasp what the man was experiencing. My racing thoughts stopped enough to register that he still held no hate in his eyes toward me for what I was doing, so I tried my best to give support to this man in his final hours.

A soldier climbed a ladder and tapped a sign on the cross above the man's head. "King of the Jews," he mocked loudly, laughing. "Crowned and standing above us all. Let's see his power now."

I felt a stirring in the air, as though angel guardians were rushing to the man's side to defend him. He stretched his fingers, signalling for them to stop, to stand down and hold themselves still even in the face of this abuse.

I had heard the man's name was Jesus. Some said he healed blind men and made the lame walk. Some said he was the Messiah. I heard that he himself said he could raise the temple of God in three days. Most mocked him, challenging him to prove he was this King the Jewish people waited for.

Suddenly darkness descended and the air grew chill. Yet it was only midday! How could this be? Strange things were happening. I knew they were significant, but I did not understand how.

In the dark, throughout the afternoon, I watched as the people who berated this man began to disperse. Only the soldiers and a few stragglers remained. Some religious men were clustered part way down the hill, not wanting to watch but apparently not able to leave, either. They seemed fearful this man would somehow free himself from my grip and leave the cross. A few women were sobbing at the foot of the cross and a young man tried to comfort them. The Centurion had ordered the soldiers to let them be, as one was the man's mother.

Jesus, whose hand I held, spoke only a few times. He told the young man to take care of his mother. He requested God's forgiveness of all around him. I was amazed.

Only once were his words to question his place of punishment. He looked to the heavens and groaned, "My God. My God. Why have you forsaken me?" Seeing his distress, the Centurion sent a soldier to offer the man a wine-soaked sponge to deaden his distress. Jesus refused, seemingly at peace again, and spoke once more in a tone of acceptance.

"It is finished."

At that moment the sun burst through the darkness and the ground trembled. I held firmly to the hand of Jesus as he gave up his spirit.

The soldiers started to run from their posts, frightened by the earthquake, but the centurion's authority halted them. I watched as the centurion gained control in the only way that worked with soldiers. He gave them an order, a task to complete. He ordered them to break the legs of the men on the crosses so they would die quicker. Their broken limbs would not be able to hold them up to take laboured breaths and they would soon suffocate.

The soldier who approached Jesus noticed he already appeared dead. To make sure, he thrust his sword into the side of the limp body and noted the fluid that poured out. I could feel the weight of Jesus pull against the secure hold of my position. Yes, he was dead.

I heard the Centurion speak in awe as he gazed at Jesus on the cross. "Surely this was the son of God." His men looked at him, concerned at their leader's strange reaction. The Centurion quickly regained his composure and commanded that the hillside be cleaned up.

A fresh group of soldiers were tasked with removing the men from the crosses. The crucified were dead, so these soldiers did not try to be gentle. They climbed ladders and tore the hands and feet of the men free of the wood, not even bothering to remove the other nails first.

When the soldier approached me and tried to pull Jesus' hand free, I gripped it tightly, unwilling to let go. I would not allow this man, strange as he was, to be disrespected in that way. Exasperated, the soldier finally grabbed me in a choke hold and pulled me away. While still upset, instead of tearing Jesus' other hand and feet free, he pulled my cohort nails from the cross as well.

Jesus' arm fell to his side as I lay on the ground in the bloodied dirt, spent from my day of work. I watched as they wrapped him in a rough blanket and a rich man claimed his body, assuring the mother he would be buried as a king and not in the field of criminals. I tried to roll onto the blanket, to remain with this man who even in death had a spirit about him that attracted me.

I had done a distasteful job, but I had done it to the best of my ability, and with compassion for the man placed in my care.

The woman, mother of Jesus, instead gathered me to her chest. I was covered in her son's blood, but she seemed not to mind, and for some reason, I did not mind either. I was covered in Jesus' blood and because of that, I knew I was forgiven for the part I played in the crucifixion. Somehow, I knew this day was important. This event would change the world and I had been a part of that. I remembered the look on Jesus' face as he urged me to my duty.

Yes, Jesus truly is the Son of God.

Torn

BY MARCIA LEE LAYCOCK

When I heard the news, I ran. My mind whirled with the impossibility of it. The curtain, the barrier that separates us all from the holy of holies, torn! Torn!

I could not imagine it. Who would do such a thing? How could they?

There was much chaos at the temple when I arrived, throngs milling about everywhere, my brother Pharisees trying to calm them, trying to calm one another.

I entered the holy place and moaned at what I saw. I stood rooted as others were, staring, dumbfounded. The curtain was indeed torn, from top to bottom. I trembled when I saw it and I too was torn, ripped from my complacency, from the comfort of ritual and tradition, torn from my will to cling to this world. I was set adrift, my anchor no longer able to hold me. For the barrier to heaven had been rent, opened undeniably, the cherubim made pointless. Why guard something that lay wide open before us?

When I took a step, everything in my being screamed at me to stop. But I took another, and another, until I was standing at the base of the curtain, the ark of the covenant before me. One more step. No, I could not go beyond. It was forbidden. Surely, I would die. And yet …

My mind filled with the image of that man on the cross, that Yeshua. The way his eyes burned into mine. In that moment was I not already torn? Torn between what I had been taught all my life and what my heart was telling me? Yes, my heart and soul were torn because when He looked at me, in that moment, I knew nothing would ever be the same. Because my heart believed. This man was the Messiah.

I took another step and fell to my knees. I joined in the moans of mourning around me until I heard a voice, like the whisper of wind in the trees, telling me to rise.

"Rise and go."

Once again, I ran, not knowing where, following that voice.

And I saw Him. By the well near my home, a crowd around Him. He smiled at me and in that moment all that was torn was mended. All the confusion, the disbelief swept away; my heart, my soul, made whole.

Yes, my world was torn apart that day. But it did not matter. In that moment, Jesus became my world, my wholeness, my righteousness. And nothing else mattered.

Through the Eyes of a Child

BY DENISE M. FORD

As I let my thoughts dwell on the Easter story, I kept seeing images of Jesus with children who, although they aren't mentioned in the scriptural Easter story, are surely there, wondering and observing what was happening. Listening and hearing, on the periphery, but still part of the story. I read the scriptures to understand how Jesus fully immersed himself in protective and tender loving actions when he became aware of children who needed him. I pictured myself as a child next to him being gathered close to him, at his feet, by his side, in his arms. Just as our loving Lord often sends his comfort to children today as they try to make sense of death, I believe Jesus drew near to those children of his time and explained his death to them in a loving and tender way.

Through the Eyes of a Child…

I squeezed through the doorway and nearly bowled over a woman kneeling in prayer as she sobbed. I tucked myself amongst the robes of a group of tall men so I could move unseen with them. I had to cover my ears as the shouting and crying rose in a crescendo. I felt dizzy as I strained to see what was happening. Then I heard his name, Jesus, Jesus.

Untangling from the robes, I felt myself falling backwards. I rolled into a ditch and pulled myself to its edge. At least I no longer could be wrenched inside by adult hands. In fact, no one seemed to notice that I had disobeyed the firm command my father had given this morning, "Stay inside today, no matter what you hear. Stay inside. Do not step beyond our doorway."

He had thrust my hand into my sister's, grabbing ours together in a firm clasp as he inhaled a long steady breath. His hands rubbed over ours, his head bent over us. I thought he would pray, but instead he breathed heavily again, embracing my mother as she came near him with my baby sister against her shoulder.

"You will stay inside today, and I will return as soon as I am able."

Then the pounding on our door had begun. My older brothers had thrown it open and practically dragged my father through it. That's when I had quickly made my escape. I didn't want to stay behind with the women. Now outside in the ditch, I wished I had followed the command to stay inside. For here before my eyes struggled the very same man I had seen riding on a donkey a few days before. I had happily weaved in and out of its plodding path joining with the joyous songs of our people. *"Hosanna, Hosanna!"* had rung out loud and clear. I had waved a palm so close to his face it had seemed that he may have laughed with me as he looked my way. He motioned for me to come closer and I eagerly ran next to him, swishing my palm alongside the donkey's hind legs. He had glanced behind and nodded as he gave another hearty laugh.

Could this be the same man? This man dragging a wooden cross before me? I scanned his face for any resemblance, but all I could see were streams of blood trickling down from a crown of thorns. His eyes… if only I could see his eyes then I would know if this man recognized me.

But people ran in front of me. Mud splattered my face and stones began to bounce as they scattered beneath a multitude of sandals. I remembered my father's warning, "Stay inside today." I closed my eyes because I no longer wanted to understand what was happening. I let the stones pummel me for a few more minutes, and then I slid from the ditch. Still trembling, I stumbled through crowds of people to make my way home, dodging past Roman soldiers, ducking under moving carts.

Back inside, I found a quiet corner and I closed my eyes. In my dream I saw him. He reached for me with a palm branch softly brushing my cheek. He nodded and gave a hearty laugh, one that I recalled from the other day. Then it felt like I was rocking gently in his arms, like he was lifting me and raising me up and up and up. I could only hear his laughter; I could only feel his love. In my dream we were next to each other; we laughed together. He stayed with me. He did not disappear underneath the weight of a heavy cross.

When I awoke again, I heard sobbing. My older brother, their wives and children, had crowded into our home. Although the voices were familiar, words that I didn't understand echoed around me. *"Brutal crucifixion... it is finished... we will all die. He's gone, it's over."* I suddenly wished I could return to this morning's commanding words, *"Stay inside. I will return when I am able."* Oh, how I wanted to return to my dream. I wanted to stay inside my dream to hear the sounds of laughter and feel the reassuring love.

So many words of death. So much weeping. No one cared where I was or even if I were still here. But somehow, I knew this man would stay with me. I had dreamt of being next to him. I had laughed with him. I had been comforted by his love. But I couldn't tell them; I was only five. I was only a child. But I knew! I knew Jesus was the man who had laughed with me, who had motioned for me to come close to him. Whose look of love I had seen again in my dream. I could only hope that he would return when he was able and that his love would stay inside me. *When I was five my Nana passed away suddenly. I found myself amidst grieving adults who spoke of things I didn't understand. One night I dreamt of Nana reaching out to me, sending me a loving look while at the same time laughing with genuine joy. Even though our minister came to answer my questions regarding death and heaven, it was this dream that brought me great comfort during this time.*

PART III
NON-FICTION

Photo by Sally Meadows

Prayer with a Side of Paska

BY PAT GERBRANDT

We were the new folks on the block. The unpainted two-storey house, our rental home, was as much a contrast to the beautifully kept, white-painted houses on either side as we were to our neighbours. The Redekopps in the newer bungalow and the Giesbrechts in the tiny cottage with its precise picket fence were both older couples. My parents were in their early forties, and I, a first-grader, had just turned six. Our neighbours were devout church-going people. We went to church only occasionally.

The Giesbrechts had moved to Canada from Russia, like most of their fellow Mennonites, to escape the harsh conditions imposed on them by a regime that did not respect their faith. It seems plausible Mrs. Giesbrecht would be concerned for people who did not give much evidence of sharing the values she and her husband held dear.

I remember one visit my mom and I made to the Giesbrechts. I remember bright sunlight streaming through the windows and reflecting on all the bright, clean surfaces of the kitchen – the cabinets, the floor, and the walls. There were no toys, but the tiny, tidy lady gave me some small leaflets. I can still remember how I enjoyed "Northern Lights" put out by Northern Canada Evangelical

Mission, serving Canada's indigenous peoples. How did Mrs. Giesbrecht know I liked reading?

Then, at Easter, Mrs. Giesbrecht brought us a delicious treat, something I'd never seen before. I am quite sure her beautiful domed Paska* with its white icing and colourful sugar sprinkles was a treat for my parents, too. It tasted as good as it looked!

I was much older when I learned the significance of that tall loaf. The loaf, rising high in the round tin, reminds us of Christ's rising from the tomb. I think the white icing suggests Christ's purity, and the sweetness of His sacrifice.

Now, as I think about the Giesbrechts' choosing faith-freedom over their former homeland, and consider the gifts of kindness they gave us, like the missionary leaflets and the Paska, I see how they fit together.

It was while we lived in that ugly old house I realized Christ's death meant I could be freed from the burden of my own sin. I didn't know to tell anyone, but my recollection of the experience is still vivid. Even I marvel! The only way it makes sense is that God gave me understanding beyond my intellectual grasp when I read John 3:16. "For God so loved the world that he gave his one and only Son, that whoever believes in him shall not perish but have eternal life."

Even though we lost touch with these neighbours after we moved to another house, their influence continues. I thank God for the kindness of that older lady and for the way her gifts still give me joy. I think she'd be very happy to know her former neighbours now share her faith. Mom learned to talk about her faith and loved to study the Bible. Daddy experienced incredible joy when he surrendered his will to the risen Christ just ten years before he died.

I believe Mrs. Giesbrecht's prayers, served up with a side of Paska, were what we as a family needed on our journey to true faith and freedom. When Easter comes, I'll be baking Paska. I like to share the lovely bread and the truth of Easter.

*The terms Paska, also called Kulich, and Babka are sometimes interchanged, although there are some differences. Both delicious breads are of Ukrainian / Eastern European origin, baked to celebrate the risen Christ.

An Easter Day Thank You

BY LYNN J. SIMPSON

My Dad sweeps his cane along the edge of the curb, a navigation lesson taught by one of his helpers from the Canadian National Institute for the Blind (CNIB). "Foot up," I command. His right foot rises, a foot that wears a size twelve, brown laced shoe. Dad's a tall man when he stands straight. He fists the black rubber of his white cane in his left hand (even though the nuns from his elementary school days forced pencils in his right hand). I wait, squinting in the mid-day sun. I hold open the Tim Horton's door. The door swung out. From experience, I'd learned the best way to navigate Dad into the narrow entry and through the double doors was for me to step up first, open the door, and then have Dad step up beside me. Now, I turn my back toward him and he reaches out his free hand, his fingers needling my shoulder before pressing his palm firmly in place. I steer us through the double doors.

He collapses his cane like a tent pole before sliding into the booth I've chosen. A bench seat seems safer somehow than tables with moving chairs. From his jacket pocket, he takes out his wallet and his fingers navigate over the inside pockets and the edges of cards until he pulls out the familiar credit card. Dad always paid. He was old-fashioned that way, some may say. Nor did he want my mother to work a job. Only that one fall season of her teaching pottery once a week to children do I remember Mom on a job. I was a child too then, and Dad supervised carpenters somewhere in Toronto on commercial construction sites. I'd hear him more than see him then. My bedroom window was above the garage door, so I'd hear the family car rumble into the driveway just before drifting to sleep. Those nights Mom kept food warm in the oven for Dad and a perfect place setting at the kitchen table with chairs we'd vacated hours before.

I leave Dad waiting at the Tim Horton's table while I purchase his coffee (a "double double"— two portions each of milk and sugar), my black coffee, and his Boston Crème donut. Back at our table, I place Dad's coffee before him, first lifting and securing the tab on his coffee lid. A Medic-Alert bracelet hangs loose on his wrist as his finger circles the plastic coffee lid, feeling for the break. Then he slides his hand down to grip the cup and finally lifts it to his pale lips. Dad looks forward to any wanderings beyond his room at the nursing home. Once he'd wandered out the doors of the home by himself, and using the skills he learned from the CNIB girls, he counted the steps to the bus bench. He heard a bus braking, and boots hitting metal, and then felt a hand grasping his, steering him on the bus and into the handicap seat. Dad didn't resist, so the story goes. He rode the route, circling back to the original bus stop where a nurse waited, relieved. And shortly thereafter, a sensor bracelet encircled my dad's right wrist to track his wanderings.

"What was the sermon about?" Dad asks. I watch him take a careful sip of his coffee.

"You were at church too. What was the sermon about?" I reply, understanding the old joke. In my teenage years I'd go alone to church when I missed the morning service with him. Dad would quiz me later on the sermon, his own way of tracking my whereabouts.

Earlier, I drove Dad to the church in his old neighbourhood. Even though church attendance was higher due to being Easter Sunday, his regular front seat was open as if waiting for his arrival only. Parishioners greeted him with taps on the shoulder and Happy Easter sentiments. At communion, the priest stepped down from the alter and gave Dad his host before positioning himself to serve the line forming. After the service, three choir members offered to help Dad into my compact rental car, wondering how long I'd be visiting in Toronto from my home in Alberta. Just one more day, I replied, positioning myself in the driver's seat. Dad's folded cane rested by his feet.

Dad had loved to drive, rarely taking rests on road trips even when Mom begged him to pull over to break from the heat of our non-air-conditioned cars. His hands steered car wheels across Canada—New Brunswick to Ottawa, Ontario to Edmonton, Alberta to Vancouver, Ontario to Whitehorse. He steered across the United States—north and south and back again. It was when he steered into a parked car on the residential street where he and mom lived that officials finally took his driver's license away. He'd been diagnosed with degenerative macular disease a few years before the accident. And like seeing a drip of coffee fallen on a photograph, his central vision gradually blackened, and grey shadows circled the edges causing blurring to his peripheral vision.

Dad's hand releases his coffee cup and slides on the table toward me. I slide the plate with his Boston Crème donut closer to him. His hand rises then drops into the chocolate coating. "Here Dad," I say, pressing a napkin into his palm. He hastily rubs away the brown stickiness with both hands. Finding the edges, he picks up the donut and takes his first bite. When he places it back on the plate a drop of crème is on his chin and a morsel of chocolate on a corner of his mouth. I lift my coffee to my dry lips.

Mom didn't take the wheel on those road trips with Dad. Mom's driving was limited to the neighbourhood Safeway or the mall, and only then when she had to. I rode the bus to all my orthodontist appointments and rode in other cars driven by other moms for dance lessons. But Mom's hands, muddy brown from clay, steered her potter's wheel. The wheel's speed, like the gas pedal of a car, dictated by the pressure of her foot on a pedal on our newspaper covered floor. Often after my bus ride from school, I'd find her in our basement, perched on her stool, hands encircling and rising and falling on spinning clay. Muddy water smeared the newsprint on the floor and spotted her glasses. "My wife's a potter," Dad would tell their friends, the double entendre revealed in the curling corners of his mouth. Later Mom's Parkinson's took command of those hands that had guided clay to become plates, vases and mugs. Her wheel was sold. Her potted creations sat in Mom and Dad's kitchen cupboards and later were packaged in brown paper since they were not needed in the nursing home.

It was the social worker that finally convinced Dad he could no longer take care of Mom. All the raised sticky dots on the oven dials, the beeping alarms on Dad's watch to indicate it was time for Mom's medication, the home care nurse and house cleaner visits were not enough against Mom's decreasing physical and mental health, and Dad's increasing frustrations. Sleep and socially deprived, Dad's patience lessened as the risks of danger grew from stove burners left on to Mom's falls in the hallways.

Dad lasted one night alone. He made the nursing home take him too, back to his wife of over 50 years, so he could be in her room on the second floor. Months later, it was when he was stroking mom's hand, he told me, when the nurse who'd just bathed and laid Mom in her bed leaned in to whisper to him, "She's gone."

Dad's found the other napkin beside his empty plate. I see the crown of his head as he wipes his mouth, wisps of grey hair falling away from his forehead. Dad drops his napkin and his chin rises as he points his first finger at me.

"Did you get that slow leak fixed on that tire you told me about?" Dad asked.

"Yes, I did."

We are silent for a minute or two, our pause like the waiting of a traffic light to change to green.

"Are you ready to go?" I ask Dad.

He says okay, slides out of the booth and leans his hands on the table, steadying himself to stand. I tap his folded cane into his left palm. I hear the click of the cane's elbows release as I step in front of him. I feel his right-hand rising on my arm. When he clutches my shoulder, I steer us out of the Tim Horton's restaurant.

After we have navigated safely through the doors and my eyes adjust to the sunlight, Dad asks, "Could we go for a drive before you take me back?"

"Sure," I reply. "How about you take the wheel this time?"

Dad snickers and pats my shoulder.

"Thank you," he says.

I wipe my eyes with one hand as the other opens the car door for Dad.

Pain and Promise

BY SYLVIA ENGEN ESPE

The day was cool and cloudy, almost mirroring the grief and heaviness of my heart. Mourning the loss of a child has to be one of life's loneliest and most painful processes. This deep devastating sorrow cut to the core of my being. I asked myself, "Is this to be another day when memories will overwhelm me and tears flow?

I could procrastinate no longer; the downstairs storeroom had to be cleaned. Easter was fast approaching, a time of the year to clean and refresh our home. "Work is great therapy," I thought to myself as I attacked the job before me. Winter boots, suitcases, and books were only a portion of the clutter in disarray concealed behind a closed door. Then to my surprise, an old Sunday School project came to view. Tucked behind jars of pickles and jam was a wall hanging that a young boy had brought home to his mother. The message, cut from leather strips in boyish fashion, simply stated, "Peace Be With You."

I immediately clasped the old leather and birch board, splintered and faded, to my bosom. Memories of a bright-eyed lad proudly presenting me with his own creation flashed before me. God's loving arms enveloped me with a sense of powerful peace. God's

Easter message of hope consoled me. Jesus was crucified on the cross that I might have life. Someday I shall be reunited with Him and our loved ones in glory!

My mind quickly drifted back several months to the night a phone call awakened me. “Mom, Wes passed away.” The hesitant voice of my daughter-in-law continued, “He had a heart attack while playing hockey. The doctors worked on him for two hours but couldn’t save his life.”

My reaction to the death of our only son was total disbelief. Wes’s father had passed away in like manner. “Oh God, you can’t take Wes away from us, too,” I cried in anguish. “Wes is only thirty-three years old, and we all need him, especially his two little children!”

I mechanically prepared for the fifty-mile trip to be with Wes’s family. The endless road loomed mockingly before me as I drove the car out into the foreboding darkness. An illusion of a never-ending tunnel in my path increased my anxiety level. I fought back tears that blurred my vision. Flickering yard lights from nearby homes taunted me as I drove by. I was perturbed and questioned, “What right do they have to shine so brightly when I am hurting to the depth of my soul?” Wes and his family had spent the weekend with us. “Wes,” I reminded myself, “You just drove on this highway less than thirty hours ago!”

I felt relief, but also fear of the unknown when I first saw the lights of Sherwood Park glimmering on the dark horizon. I dreaded arriving at my son’s home. He wouldn’t be there to welcome me with open arms. There would no longer be the hope of any denial on my part. I would be forced to accept the fact that my son would no longer help me with my bookkeeping, nor be the entertainer at our family gatherings, or be my support and cheerleader. Silent streets led me to the home with the newly built double garage. “The first garage I’ve built, Mom!” Wes’s words of pride echoed in my memory.

Sleepless hours moved slowly as a daughter-in-law and mother sat in total disbelief. "This can't be! How can we cope without a loving son, husband, and father?" Two little children slept soundly in an adjacent room, oblivious to the loss of their beloved Daddy.

We were startled in our grief by the ringing of the doorbell. Victim Services, represented by a teacher and an administrator who sacrificed their night's sleep, brought compassion and understanding to a distraught audience. They remained with us at length, seemingly reluctant to leave two ladies, both in shock, alone. We were consoled by their extended presence with us.

The chimes of the clock upstairs interrupted my reverie. I again pressed the old leather and birch hanging lovingly to me. I was reminded of the first Easter Sunday, reminded of the women who found the tomb empty after Jesus was crucified. Matthew 28:5-7 (NIV) tells us, *"The angel said to the women, Do not be afraid, for I know that you are looking for Jesus, who was crucified. He is not here. He has risen, just as he said. Come and see the place where he lay. Then go quickly and tell his disciples. He has risen from the dead and is going ahead of you into Galilee. There you will see him. Now I have told you."*

This Easter message spoke to me. It brought me a sense of peace and promise that touched my heart. Jesus asked these women to spread the joy of the resurrection. We, too, are to tell others the news that God's Son lives. We can be assured that Jesus, just as He promised, rose from the dead. Death is not the end.

God met me in the storeroom that day with a blessed surprise. God's Easter message of hope became gloriously mine. Life goes on. Each day is a gift from God. I try to remember, when I experience sad and lonely days, that I was blessed to have had Wes as a loving son, even for a short time. I know Wes is at peace. The gift of life is still mine. I thank God for His promise of continued presence until I, too, join my Saviour and loved ones in glory. I am blessed!

Aunt Pauline and The Little Easter

BY ALLISON LYNN

My Aunt Pauline was the life of the party. She told the best jokes, cooked way too much food, and embraced everyone with the love of a mother hen sweeping chicks under her wing. No matter how far away we moved, visiting her was always like going home. Everyone loved her. Literally, everyone. If you met her, you'd love her, too.

She always asked us to sing. Every visit. Without fail.

My aunt was a lifelong church choir singer, so she was always incredibly supportive of my singing. When my husband, Gerald, and I started our music ministry together, she became one of our biggest fans. Whenever we traveled home to Newfoundland for a concert tour, Aunt Pauline and Uncle Melvin would be there in the front row, beaming with pride and singing along.

She was just the best of everything.

But a few years ago, we started to notice small changes in her demeanour. Odd behaviours, forgetfulness—something was different. The sickening descent of dementia was taking my aunt away from us, one tiny step at a time.

As the months and years unfolded, it became harder for my uncle to care for his bride. In the bleakness of winter, she finally made the move into the hospital. It didn't need to be said. We all knew she'd never come home again.

When Gerald and I traveled to Newfoundland that spring, we knew this would be a different kind of visit. We sat by Aunt Pauline's bedside, chatting with my uncle and their many visitors. She smiled at me, and tried to join in the storytelling and joking. We didn't know if she was following any of it, but we were thankful for her quick and easy laughter.

On our final day, we made one last trip to the hospital. We hugged Uncle Melvin, as he gave us a little time to spend with Aunt Pauline.

She was quiet that day. She smiled weakly, barely meeting my eyes. I couldn't tell if she recognized us. "Gerald brought his guitar. Would you like us to sing for you?" Gerald stood at the end of the bed. I sat in the chair beside her. We began to sing, and her eyes brightened as we started the familiar words, "Be Thou my vision, O Lord of my heart…"

As the final chord rang out, Gerald looked at me, "Why don't you sing 'In The Garden' for her?"

I moved my chair even closer, so Aunt Pauline could hear my voice, feel my words. I held her hand. Gerald played a sweet introduction. I began, "I come to the garden alone, while the dew is still on the roses…"

Line after line, singing of that first Easter morning. Mary arrives at the tomb, heartbroken by the death of her beloved Rabbi. The light and the love that she knew had been sealed in a tomb forever. This wasn't the way she thought it would end.

Until she heard the voice … that voice … that familiar, loving voice ….

"And He walks with me and He talks with me, and He tells me I am His own…"

At that moment, Aunt Pauline's lips began to move. She was singing!

Just like Mary, I was hearing a familiar voice, a voice that I thought had been lost to me forever.

Deep in her memory, the music was moving, stirring her soul. My Aunt Pauline had been sealed in a tomb of illness and pain, but a mere tomb is no match for the source of all life. Decades before, Jesus had come to live in my aunt's heart, and now, freed by lyric and melody, that life was shining through!

Right there in that hospital bed, we had our own little Easter.

A glimpse of glory.

A reawakening of eternal life.

The whole world stopped as Aunt Pauline and I sang to each other. I couldn't take my eyes off my beautiful aunt. This was going to be our final moment together, and I didn't want to miss a breath of it.

Her eyes were full of life and joy! Mine were burning with tears, but I refused to let them fall. I dug my nails into my leg to stop myself from crying. I didn't want her to think I was upset. She was giving me such a gift of love, and I wanted to do the same for her.

We sang these perfect, fitting final words together, "And the joy we share, as we tarry there, none other has ever known."

The final notes drifted through the room as we sat in the stillness, hands clasped. I looked into those eyes that had loved me my whole life. I could barely see straight for the flood of memories filling the air.

"You're such a lovely singer," I said to her, and she laughed. I kissed her and kissed her and kissed her again. Gerald kissed her and we said our goodbyes. As we walked down the hall, Gerald held my hand as I finally let the tears fall down my face.

A few weeks later, Aunt Pauline's church choir stood around her bedside to serenade her with folk songs and hymns, including "In The Garden." In the quiet moments after midnight, Aunt Pauline died peacefully, surrounded by her family, enveloped in prayer.

I can only imagine her arrival in Heaven was a joyful one, filled with laughter and singing.

Now, whenever I sing "In the Garden," I think of my Aunt Pauline. I remember that glimpse of glory we experienced in her hospital room. I know that the love that lives in each of us can be temporarily buried but never stopped. We carry the power of the Resurrection deep in our hearts, and so we can experience this truth every day of our lives:

God wins! Life wins!

I'm forever grateful for that little Easter.

Our Easter Story

BY L. MARIE ENNS

Would she even live long enough to get that transplant? Her body was literally wasting away day after day as we waited for the phone call to give us a surgery date. Her liver was functioning so poorly that what little food she could eat was doing her no good.

As our daughter was growing up, we had no idea she had a rare liver disease. It was discovered only when she was in nurses' training. From then on it was monitored and in time had to be controlled by medication.

Laurella was married, finished her RN training, had two sons, and later went back to work. Her liver was deteriorating, and after some years, the day came when she was too ill to continue her nursing career. The only solution was to have a transplant.

Finally, the transplant was done shortly before Easter in March, 2008. We were allowed to see Laurella just before she was taken to the operating room. I was surprised at how peaceful she was. She was sitting up in her bed, calmly knitting, as she waited to go into surgery.

On Easter weekend, Laurella's husband, Brett, and sons, Brynn and Kieran, were in Vancouver with her, and my husband, Henry, and I were in Abbotsford. We attended a morning Easter service with our son, Lyndell, and his family, and then had dinner with them.

That afternoon Lyndell took us to Vancouver to see Laurella in the hospital and have a little Easter service with her. She took us to a small room where we wouldn't disturb other patients. She was able to walk slowly, with her brother assisting her with her IV pole. Laurella asked us to sing, "Christ the Lord Is Risen Today." We did the best we could without musical accompaniment and with mixed emotions. Yes, we were rejoicing in Christ's resurrection and also in Laurella's successful transplant, but we were still painfully aware that we could have lost her if that surgery had been delayed longer.

Laurella was to stay in Vancouver for the first months of her recovery. First, she stayed in the hospital and then in a rented suite with Brett taking care of her. Henry went home to attend to his real estate business and I kept our grandsons company in their home on Vancouver Island as they continued attending school. On some weekends we took the ferry to visit Laurella and Brett. Other Sundays we attended their church in North Saanich.

Laurella was recovering well for about four weeks, but then suddenly, her condition grew worse. Something had gone gravely wrong. A bile leak had damaged her liver ducts and caused a raging infection. It was not at all certain that her new liver would keep functioning. She was placed into intensive care and given drugs to fight the infection.

The next weekend, the boys and I went to see her. I told Brett he might as well spend some time with his sons and I would sit with Laurella. It was more difficult than I had thought. I had never seen anyone in the ICU before, and I was not prepared for all the tubes and machines attached to my daughter. The machines beeped and numbers fluctuated. I felt alarmed because I didn't know what it all meant. Laurella looked even more ill than I had ever seen her before and the drugs kept her sedated. She couldn't have talked in any case, with a tube down her throat. At one point she roused a bit, opened her eyes, and motioned with her hands, but neither her nurse nor I could understand what she wanted.

The boys and I returned to the Island on Sunday night so they could be in school on Monday. That day we got word that another liver had been found for Laurella after she had been put on the Canada-wide list. Her first transplant had been from a live donor, but now the ducts were ruined, so she had to have a whole new liver.

By now, her body was even weaker than for the first transplant, but she had to have the second transplant to save her life. With many people praying for her, she survived the surgery and began her slow recovery, with the new liver functioning well. Her body had a hard time adjusting to food again, but eventually she was able to start eating. On a weekend visit near the end of April, we took her a package of many birthday cards from her church friends.

Laurella was allowed to come home for a few days in June to attend Brynn's High School Graduation. She was still weak and had to go in a wheelchair. She was so emaciated that some of her friends didn't recognize her. After spending more time in Vancouver, she was allowed to come home to stay at the end of June. By this time, she was eating well. Soon after that, I returned home to Saskatchewan.

I didn't see my daughter for many months until she was well enough to come and see us. When she walked into our house, I was amazed at her transformation! I had my daughter back! She looked so well and healthy, as if she had never had a medical problem. It was like a resurrection! Praise be to our Lord, the Great Physician!

After seeing that miracle of restoration, it is not hard to believe that God will be able to resurrect us from our graves with new bodies and take us to Heaven. This is possible because Jesus died and was resurrected for us, so that if we repent and believe in Him, we will also rise to eternal life when He comes to take us home. In John 14:19, Jesus promised His disciples,

"Because I live, you also will live."
Christ the Lord is risen indeed. Alleluia!

Easter Now and Then

BY ANGELINA FAST-VLAAR

Coffee in one hand, phone in the other, I set out on an Easter morning walk around a park – my favourite route. It's chilly – sky is grey. I'm glad the cup warms one gloved hand. A lone runner approaches, moves off the sidewalk to let me pass at six foot distance. We smile a COVID good-morning greeting.

Mom's soft knock on our bedroom door.

"Girls – time to go!"

We don our Easter dresses, take along a sweater – just in case. At seventeen, I take the wheel, drive down the winding River Road to Oaks Park in a near-by town. We come upon a happy gathering of musicians, singers, observers. Excited, we climb the bleachers.

"Not too high!"

"Half-way up, OK?"

The sun – also climbing – crests the horizon, bathing us in light. Magnificent! Majestic!

A path leads into the park. Swings and slides now sadly imprisoned in fencing and yellow caution tape. Five benches tucked here and there upon green grass. Not allowed to congregate – but all alone? I choose a favourite, sheltered under a tree struggling to sprout leaves.

A deep breath. I treasure the stillness. Mary came to the garden – was it also chilly that morning? She looked into the empty tomb – chilling for sure. But there's an angel! There's a message! He has risen! Unbelievable! Best to ask this stranger where they've placed Him.

"Mary."

One word – equal to a thousand! And then:

"Go tell! Go tell the men, go tell my disciples, go tell my brothers…"

And she did.

I grasp the cup with my other hand.

High on the bleachers, basking in the rising sun, we listen as musicians fill the park with joyful strains. We join the chorus – voices blending in the morning light, echoing into streets around us:

"He has risen! He has risen indeed!"

The message ever joyful, everlasting.

We're loath to leave, but slowly find our way midst the descending throng.

"Wasn't that just so lovely?"

"It was marvelous. So glad we went!"

Our new country is a good place! Home, school, work, family, and peace, yes peace after war. And even a car to drive to a sun-rise service!

I adjust my phone. Andrew is preaching. He relates the Easter story – the first words Jesus spoke to gathered followers: "Peace be with you."

Peace – despite the turmoil of the times in Jerusalem. Peace – despite this present COVID tumult.

The wind picks up – best to saunter home. Turning right, I pass a church. Deserted. No one will gather here today. I settle on the steps – a moment's shelter from the western wind.

Shelter – a word laden with meaning. Mom with her arm around me as we huddled in a shelter made to protect us from falling bombs. God sheltered Noah in the ark, Elijah at the brook, Hagar in the desert … God promises shelter beneath his wings.

"I will take refuge in the shadow of your wings until the disaster has passed." (Ps. 57:1)

Yes, shelter promised during this disastrous COVID time.

Soft light now spreads across the eastern sky. He has risen. He is present. My step is somewhat lighter as I venture home to shelter in place on this Easter day.

PART IV
POETRY

Photo by Marnie Pohlman

A Pearl of Great Value

BY ALVIN ENS

Again, the kingdom of heaven is like a merchant
searching for fine pearls Mt. 15:45 NET Bible

If we go beyond everyday experience
only the privileged few
have seen and touched, much less owned
a pearl of great value

Pearls – the beauty
scarcity, rarity
elusiveness, mystery
value and worth

To the skeptic – a vain pursuit
to the cynic – a temporary bauble
to the doubting – unattainable happiness
to the critic –valueless, worthless

Perhaps that's the point
the kingdom of heaven
is beyond everyday experience
an esoteric Easter experience for the few

Search ceaselessly for fine pearls
find one of great value
sell everything you own
to obtain it

Now and Forever

BY CAROL MACKAY

I cannot find Him in most books I've read,
the shows I have watched, in the injustices lauded,
marching, booting down our streets.
Even touchdown praises have shifted away
to the glory of something other.
Roll it away, that stone.
Roll it away, so the corners may be lit.
That stone must roll away.
Even with the world's wasting words,
even as corners darken,
even without touchdown praises,
even if injustices are applauded and
they are untrue to his name,
it remains so, now, and forever,
that stone was rolled away.

Communion

BY MARNIE POHLMANN

I remember
as a child,
learning stories of the beginnings,
God's care through generations,
the need for sacrifice.

I remember
short weeks ago
celebrating by lighted evergreen
the birth of Messiah,
Promise fulfilled.

I remember
as though it were today,
receiving Christ's gift of Blood
cleansing my heart,
giving me hope.

I remember.
So today,
with others who believe,
I pause—Selah
I remember.

Remembering Easter

BY PATRICIA A. EARL

T'was the night before Easter and all over town
Folks were busy preparing as business shut down.
The kids, all excited would not close an eye
Wishing that night would quickly pass by.
Mom in the kitchen was baking some bread
And Dad coloured eggs to hide under the bed.
There was silver to polish, the table to set,
Flowers to arrange for the party, and yet,
Something was missing, now what could that be?
Celebrations seemed hollow, despite all the glee.

Across town a pastor knelt by a pew,
"Lord, please let the town's folk know it's all about You.
It's not about rabbits or new clothes to wear,
Or having a party with relatives there.
It's not about spring or lilies so white,
It's not about chocolate eggs you can bite.
You are the reason that Easter is here,
The cross now is empty and we need not fear.
Please open their eyes and give them a reason
To celebrate rightly this Easter season."

Back at the house, Mom paused for a rest,
The house was pristine, she had done her best.
She stood by the window and gazed at the moon,
The night was far gone, the dawn would come soon.
T'was then she remembered a far bygone day
When at Easter her family all made their way
To the church on the hill, where they sang and they prayed
And rejoiced at the empty tomb where Jesus was laid.
With tears in her eyes and a heart full of love,
She took time to talk to the Father above.
Tomorrow they would go to the church on the hill,
And for a few moments of time, would be still,
To focus on Easter and the freedom God gives,
To sing Hallelujah! All praise! Jesus lives!

The Easter Hallelujah

JOCELYN FAIRE

D*o not abandon yourselves to despair. We are the Easter people and hallelujah is our song.* — Pope John Paul II (Karol Wojtyła)

The Easter Hallelujah

I am the song of Easter
Many voices add fullness to my tune
My anthem began before the creation of the world
It took shape and form as the earth was birthed
It wandered the wilderness in search of a homeland
It has been the aching of the ages
It became visual with the birth of a baby...
a special child who grew in favour in the eyes of the Lord
a special child who was the Lord.

I am the song of the seasons
The praises formed in the heat of summer
The harvest song of a well lived life
The frozen anguish in the dead of winter,
The irrepressible burst of green life in spring.
I am the song of celebration

The song of beauty.

I am the song of despair... the longing song
How long, oh Lord, will you hide your face from us?
I am the song of confusion
Afraid to trust the melody when the notes are unclear
I am the song of plenty and the song of want
The lament of pain, the balm of comfort
I am the song of amnesia,
Words forgotten in the dark of night
I am the song of light and memory
Sing this in remembrance of me.

I am the voice in the crowd... joining the Hosanna of Palm Sunday...
I am the same voice in the crowd calling Crucify him! Crucify him!
I am the song of silent shame
And I am the song of grace and forgiveness
I am the song of strong surrender
The song that hung rugged on the cross...

I am the song of power... the resurrection power that lives within
I am the song of hope... green seeded hope that overflows
Hope to join loved ones again
I am the song of rest, abide in me, sing my lullaby
I am the song within your heart
Come let us make a joyful noise unto the Lord.

We join the song, with voices weak or strong...
This is the song of humanity
This is the song of a God who sings over us in the night
This is the song of gratitude, of praise, of sorrow
This is a song unstoppable.

And centuries later I am the receiver of this song
At the graveside of a son, a daughter, a loved one
and I can barely whisper...
we do not grieve as those who have no hope
Others carry the tune which I cannot hold
The spirit sings to aching hearts around the world.

Will you join the song of a broken Hallelujah?

Easter Walk

BY MARCIA LEE LAYCOCK

The white shawl of winter is
being drawn back
revealing the bare shoulders
of a still cold land.

They are dark with moisture and
grey trees peer over them in silence,
ripe with yearning for green
and the lilt of summer birds.

And as I walk I joy to hear
the soft trickle of
winter's undoing,
the flow of life beginning again.

I stop, stoop down
pick up a stone patterned
by two dark lines,
vertical, horizontal.

My thumb traces the cross.

Yes. Life
beginning again.

Palm Sunday

BY CONNIE MAE INGLIS

Look—the King is here.
Hosanna! Hosanna!
Look—the King is your salvation.
Hosanna! Hosanna!

Look—not at the palm branches,
  green but for a moment,
  then brown with death—No.
Look at the palms of Jesus,
  humanity in the flesh,
  divinity in the scars, death
  but for a moment, then life
  for eternity.

Look at the palms of blood.
Look—in faith, and believe;
  in love, and surrender;
  in hope, and trust.

Look—Jesus is your Salvation.
Hosanna! Hosanna!

The Night Before Easter

BY PATRICIA A. EARL

T'was the night before Easter and all through the town
Not a creature was stirring, there wasn't a sound.
The children were sleeping, innocent and still
Dreaming sweet dreams as most children will;
While mother and father, their mats near the door,
Fearfully wondered what tomorrow held in store.

Out on a hill near a cave cold and black
A soldier stood guard, a large stone at his back.
He thought of events that had happened that day,
Remembering scenes he had passed on his way;
Loud crowds on the roads, fists raised, tempers hot,
Pilate, the governor, appease them could not.
He offered Barabbas, a thief, all round cur,

They cheered, "Pass him over, he's our man for sure!"
"But what will I do with the man you call Jesus?"
"Crucify Him! Crucify Him! That's how you can please us!"

The guard shook his head, he could not understand
How the fate of another could rest in one hand.
He recalled the large cross hewn from olive wood trees
On the back of a man who collapsed to His knees.
How soldiers, when prodding failed, turned to the crowd,
Barking their orders in tones harsh and loud:
"Simon! You, Simon. Come carry the cross!
Hurry up, man, enough time has been lost!"
The crowd surged forward to the top of the hill,
Soon hammer and nail mixed with screams loud and shrill.

As he recalled, he shuddered and sighed
For on that very spot, three men had died.
He felt rather ashamed as the scene crossed his mind,
His colleague's coarse comments had been most unkind.
Casting lots for His cloak - that was stooping low
And a sponge soaked in wine, hoping death would be slow.

He recalled then the words that were spoken so clear

The voice from the centre cross, strong, without fear,
"Father forgive them for what they don't know
It's Your will I'm doing. You do love them so."
He took one last breath, "it's finished and done.'
The centurion marvelled–"He was surely God's Son!"

The earth shook and trembled, the sun disappeared,
Darkness descended and all people feared.
A rich man called Joseph offered his tomb,
For Jesus the Christ he would always make room.
And now, here he stood to keep thieves away;
These Jews were afraid of a body of clay!

Perhaps there was more to this Man than he knew,
But for now, in the silence, one thing was true,
Death had the victory; Jesus lay in the cave,
He would do his duty, Roman face to save.
The night before Easter silence filled the land;
The day's events fulfilling God's holy plan.

Broken

BY CAROL ELAINE HARRISON

Crimson etched eyes
Tear streaked cheeks
Uninvited anger
Pouncing unannounced
Strangling all hope
And I'm screaming
Can't go on?
Go on?

Battered broken
Shoulders droop
Bowed under heavy weights
Tentacles of fear
Overpower
And I cry out
How long Lord?
How long?

Bruised and broken
Shoulders bowed
Under sin's crushing weight

earth shakes rocks crumble
Darkness descends
And He cries out
It's finished
Finished

Whispering words
Invite me
Find rest from your burdens
Drop desperation
Before the cross
And I cry out
Have mercy
Mercy

Arms lifted up
Cleansed transformed
New creation in Christ
Freed from sin and guilt
My eyes sparkle
And I'm singing
Praise the Lord
Praise Him.

The Veil Was Torn

BY KIMBERLEY PAYNE

Hang the curtain from the clasps and place the ark of the covenant law behind the curtain. The curtain will separate the Holy Place from the Most Holy Place (Exodus 26:33).

Hung between
the Holy Place and
the Most Holy Place.
A symbol.
The separation of sinful man from
the presence of God.
God's protection.
A barrier.
Until sin could be atoned for.
One allowed to enter
the Most Holy Place.
Once a year.
Made of cloth
thick as a man's hand.
Thirty feet wide.
Sixty feet long.

With a loud cry, Jesus breathed his last. The curtain of the temple was torn in two from top to bottom (Mark 15:37–38).

One clean rip.
Privilege.
To enter the presence of the King of kings,
the Lord of lords.
A visible gesture.
Declaring passage
into the Most Holy Place.

Therefore, brothers and sisters, since we have confidence to enter the Most Holy Place by the blood of Jesus, by a new and living way opened for us through the curtain, that is, his body (Hebrews 10:19–20).

The curtain torn.
For me.
For you.
Jesus' death
gave way
to our life.

The Great I Am

BY CARAN JANTZEN

Sacrificial Lamb, the great I Am
Stretched out across a tree
Nails driven deep
Torn flesh weeps
His blood poured out for me

Crucified Lamb, the great I Am
Lifted high for all to see
His willing choice
Their mocking voice
Come down and we'll believe

Slaughtered Lamb, the great I Am
His body lifted off the tree
In final breath
He conquered death
Sin's curse has been defeated

Risen Lamb, the great I Am
Lifted high for all to see
With arms stretched wide

By Father's side
He is waiting patiently

Almighty Lamb, the great I Am
Returning for all to see
With lightning flash
And trumpet blast
He will come victoriously

Little lamb, do you know I Am?
He alone can set you free
Free from sin's grasp
From death at last
If only you believe

That First Easter

CAROL ELAINE HARRISON

That First Easter
And the rough-hewn beams drip
with crimson drops
As noon day's sky turns ink-black
like midnight
Earth shudders in turmoil
crumbling rocks

And this Jesus cries out "It is finished!"

His body wrapped, buried
in borrowed tomb
As bewildered fearful followers
flee

Third day dawns
weeping women discover
Rolled away stone
men in shining garments
Proclaiming
He is not here

He's alive.

Easter

BY ALVIN ENS

Arms outstretched in papal blessing
He hangs, a silhouette
against the ashen sky
all the religious at his trial
few at his execution
fewer yet at his burial
embalmed, shrouded, sealed
a finale

till epilogue so mighty
became a swelling prologue
to history's parade of saints
reversal so complete
dark Friday became good
and the week's first day
a celebration of resurrection

Easter worship attended
annually by all the religious
fewer at weekly first day remembrance
fewer yet about His work
His arms remain outstretched

Kingdom Come

BY JANET SKETCHLEY

Design by Janet Sketchley

From Grief to Joy

BY L. MARIE ENNS

Mourning Mother Mary—
They killed her innocent Son
Despondent, devastated disciples—
Their Master lies lifeless, entombed
Godly, grieving women take spices
To anoint their Lord's body—
Their final act of kindness.
Hope dashed by despair
Faith weakened by perplexity
Joy crushed by sorrow
The atmosphere hangs heavy
With grief and gloom,
Disappointment and dismay.

Then Sunday morning
Resurrection bursts forth!
The tomb is empty
New hope is born
On Easter morn
Joy and faith return
As confused minds struggle

To wholly comprehend
This new, unexpected revelation
Jesus is alive again!
He has risen from the dead
He has died and risen as He said
Glory to God in the highest
Alleluia! Christ is risen
Indeed!

Psalm of Mary Magdalene

BY VALERIE RONALD

You told me in Galilee this would happen to you.
Suffering, rejection, death -- rising up?
Forgive the doubt which deafened me.
I did not want to know what bitter cup you had to drink.
You only spoke another parable, so I told myself.

Story became cruel truth when I saw you nailed to a cross,
Your arms stretched taut in agony, never to embrace again.
I watched and wept distraught through midday gloom
As you were torn from me like a veil from my face.

Those many days I walked beside you,
Prepared your food, sat with you by firelight,
I did not know your body held my own Messiah,
My deliverer from demons, discerner of my thoughts.
All I knew was that you loved me.

When I saw your lifeless body laid in a tomb, you were lost to me.
Myrrh and aloes imbued with tears, my last offering.
Death rolled its stone between us,
Crushed all but memories of how you loved.

In mourning I came sleepless through gray dawn
To your empty grave awash in angel light.
"He is not here; he has risen!" they told me.
I cried until you said my name.
My heart knew, before my eyes beheld you.

I was the first to see your wounded feet walk again,
Once cold in death, now warm beneath my hands.
Behind me gaped your empty tomb.
Love stood before me, whole, alive.
I should have known, Rabboni, you would find a way.

PART V
FICTION

"Victory" by Lorilee Guenter

Easter in the Snow

BY EUNICE COOPER-MATCHETT

Abby stared out the kitchen window. Snow spiralled off the roof and formed little whirlwinds between the back fence and her house. The thermometer on the post registered minus thirty degrees Celsius. Her throat tightened. How could this be possible? It was Good Friday and well past mid-April. Winter had lost its mind.

She wandered into the dining room where she'd lined up four plastic baskets filled with Easter goodies. A gust of wind hit the patio doors, making them rattle in their frame. She glanced at the heavy gray skies. Mike the weatherman, was right. There was no sign of the storm letting up. Her eyes misted. Without a weather miracle there would be no family Easter this year.

Abby had given up making holiday celebrations several years ago, more than happy to pass the privilege onto her daughter, but this year felt different. She'd suffered a heart attack in February, and according to her doctor and family, it had been touch and go for a few weeks, but God hadn't seen fit to take her home yet. *He still has something for me to do down here*, she'd told herself.

Maybe that's why making Easter dinner one last time was so important to her, but she wasn't sure. All she knew is she *had* to do it. And with the holiday coming late this year it would be perfect.

The children could play outside, making less commotion indoors, and her daughter and daughter-in-law were bringing the meal trimmings. All she needed to do was roast the turkey and ham. She thought of them lying in the freezer, begging to be taken out and enjoyed. Her throat tightened for the second time in as many minutes. Probably not going to happen.

She sank onto her couch and picked up her Bible. Blizzards or tornados never kept God away, and for this she was thankful. She opened the well-worn Book to a passage she'd relied on so heavily over the years. *Ask and ye shall receive*. Her faith in those few words had put boots on her children's feet and coats on their backs when there was no money in the bank account. She smiled, marveling at some of the most unusual and unbelievable sources of these blessings. God had never left her without. Except when he took James.

The day He'd taken her husband had been a warm, early, spring day. Ice covered the sidewalks and streets, making it suicidal to consider venturing outside. And nobody in their right mind would do so, but their son, James Junior had been teething, and all the adversities that go with the territory happened. Including running out of diapers.

"I'll walk to Walmart," James offered. "It's not safe to take the car, but those ice grips I've never used that slip over boots are in the closet. I'll give them a try." With that, he shrugged into his coat, put on his boots with the grips, and was out the door. "See you in half an hour." The door banged behind him.

A shudder had passed through Abby, but she shrugged it off when J.J. started fussing in her arms. She curled her index finger and let him bite on the knuckle. Right away he quietened and she lay him in his crib and began washing the two-hour-old supper dishes. When the last pot was tucked away in its place she checked on the baby, finding him sound asleep.

She'd glanced at her watch. She still remembered doing so after all these years. James should have been home. The shudder she'd experienced earlier wormed into her thoughts, and she very cautiously penguin-walked out to the street and looked down the sidewalk to see if there was any sign of him.

Two intersections away red and blue lights flashed. Her breath caught. The earlier shudder exploded into dread and she knew. She just knew. And she'd been right.

A tear that had spilled down her cheek turned cold, bringing her back to the present. She took a deep breath and swallowed the sobs that so badly wanted to manifest themselves and prayed the same prayer she'd prayed for twenty-five years. *Why, God? Did you need him more than we did?*

She set her Bible, still open, on the couch beside her and strolled to the hallway where all the wedding pictures hung on the wall. She stared at hers and James'. They'd had so many hopes and dreams. All unfulfilled except two precious children. How long she stood there, she couldn't say. All she knew was the house had darkened. A glance out the window told her that although it had darkened outside, the snow had stopped.

It needed shovelling. She'd told the young boy who'd faithfully cleared her walk all winter she didn't need him anymore, so that left only one option. Without another thought, she donned her coat, hat, and gloves, and stepped out into the bitter evening air. She'd only do the front sidewalk where people walked. The back would melt as soon as spring returned. In ten minutes, the walkway was void of snow. Thank the Lord it was powdery, rather than the normal spring heavy stuff, but still her heart pounded until her chest hurt and her legs felt wobbly.

Her well-worn, dusty rose recliner sat angled to the television, and grasping the arm of her couch, then the back of her desk chair for support, she made it to the easy chair and collapsed into it. Clinging to her burning chest, she closed her eyes. *Is it my turn now*? she prayed. *Do I finally get to see James again?*

She listened, waiting for that still, small voice but it never came. Neither did the pain in her chest intensify. Slowly it ebbed, leaving her weak and tired. "I guess it's not my time after all," she muttered aloud, then leaned back and closed her eyes.

Bright sunbeams flooded through the window, forcing Abby awake, but her sensitive eyes stayed closed until they adjusted to the light. Excitement flooded through her. It was Easter Saturday and the sun was shining. Maybe Easter dinner would happen after all. Once her eyes adjusted, she glanced around. Where was she? Every joint in her body, and some she didn't even realize she had, ached. Then it all came back. The storm. The shovelling. Her fatigue.

She pushed out of the chair and stood on wobbly legs until she regained her equilibrium, then made her way to the washroom. When she emerged, the phone was ringing and she hurried to answer it before it hung up.

"Hi Mom." Her daughter's strained voice greeted her. "Can you see your neighbour's house across the street?"

She walked to the window. "Of course. And the sun has turned my winter wonderland into a diamond covered landscape."

He daughter made a strange sound. Not a laugh, but not a groan either. Just something in between. "Not so here. There's a full blown blizzard raging. The drifts are so high we're going to be snowed in for a week, which means J.J. and Tina will be as well." The sobs she seemed to have been fighting broke. "I'm so sorry, Mom. I know how much tomorrow meant to you, but we can still do it as soon as the weather permits."

Disappointment beyond description washed through Abby and she fought not to join her daughter's sobs. She wilted into her recliner. And to think, she was about to take a turkey and ham out of the freezer. They exchanged a few more words before ending the conversation. Abby glanced around her empty house. She couldn't even hug Sebastian, her old orange tom cat. He'd passed away two years ago. Now, she was completely alone. The first time she'd spent Easter by herself in all her sixty-odd years.

Are you really by yourself?

Despite her aching joints, Abby leapt to her feet and looked around. "Hello? How did you get in here?"

Silence replied.

Abby wiped her perspiring brow. She'd heard someone as plain as if they'd been sitting on her couch. She wilted back into her chair. This couldn't be happening. No dementia existed in her family tree.

Her open Bible remained on the couch where she'd left it yesterday and she retrieved it. Whatever or whoever she'd heard was right. She wasn't alone. God had been with her through all those lonely nights after the children were tucked into their beds or at youth group or just hanging with their friends. Then, they left to start their own families, but God had remained.

She flipped through the tattered pages and stopped at a familiar high-lighted verse. *Be content in all things*. As she reminisced on situations she'd needlessly fretted about over the years, that familiar *peace that passes all understanding* seeped into her. She'd been behaving like an undisciplined child. Military families would be separated half a world apart, nurses would be on duty, and she was whining over nothing. Tomorrow would be just fine. "FaceTime" was a lovely invention she'd forgotten to consider. So what if the children got their baskets later? She smiled. This way, they'd still have more goodies after the original ones were just memories. She leaned back and sighed. Yes, contentment was a lovely thing.

Easter Sunday, a three-foot snowdrift blocked her garage door, making it impossible to attend church, but Abby's heart still smiled. She turned on the television to her favourite pastor who'd gotten her through her heart-attack days when she'd been too ill to leave home. Two services lasted until noon.

As if knowing they were finished, her iPad chimed. When she answered it, her daughter's smiling face filled the screen, then her family joined her. The children laid out all the contents of their Easter baskets on the coffee table. "Grammy, see what we got," they chimed in unison. "The Easter bunny found us."

Abby laughed, wishing she were with them, but she was still content to spend her day with the one who made this day special two thousand years ago. "Now, don't you eat it all at once, or you'll spoil your dinner."

"We won't." The children disappeared from the screen and Abby chatted with Janet and Tom about a second Easter celebration.

The doorbell chimed, startling all three. "One minute." Abby held up her finger. "I'll be right back."

She opened her front door.

Two other widows from her Bible study group stood on her front step, both weighed down with steaming bowls and foil covered platters. "Our families can't make it home," Margaret, the older lady explained, "so we decided a three strand cord is stronger together than each one by itself. We're here to enjoy an Easter feast."

Abby's eyes blurred. God had seen her misery — again — and sent her what she needed. She swallowed hard, opened the door wider, and gestured for her friends to enter. "Come in. I'll just say goodbye to my daughter."

Janet smiled when Abby picked up her iPad. "I heard all that. You go enjoy dinner with friends and we'll do Easter when the weather agrees with spring. I'll let J.J. know you have company so he'll wait until evening to chat."

"Thank you, and I love you," Abby whispered before ending their chat. She stepped into the kitchen where her friends were busy unwrapping bowls and platters. Gratitude overwhelmed her. God had seen her loneliness again and met her in the midst of it. Her mouth watered from the aroma filling her tiny kitchen.

When the food was spread out on the table and the three ladies took their seats, Abby bowed her head. "Thank you, Father God, for this bountiful feast, good friends, your favour, and patience with this impatient old lady who seems to complain before remembering your goodness."

The Placement of the Cross

BY SALLY MEADOWS

Lucy and I walked through the dim church hallway, the coolness a respite from the unexpectedly warm April sunlight streaming into our classroom. It was an impromptu decision to spend some one-on-one time with my delightful student who had special needs, and I relished the opportunity. Meaghan, Lucy's educational assistant, remained back at the classroom, getting her own break from routine by leading an art class with the other students.

Lucy, as always, had her colourful My Little Pony collection clutched to her chest. As a child with cognitive delays and autism, she didn't speak much. But when she tugged on my sleeve and looked up at me with her big brown eyes—magnified by her thick-lensed purple glasses—I knew she had something important to say. I knelt down, encouraging her to speak.

Stumbling over her words—as she often did—she squeaked out, "I saw the cross."

I stood up, surprised and perplexed. Lucy pointed to the dark alcove we had just passed. I peered inside, my eyes squinting. There, tucked against the back wall, was a large wooden cross. With Lucy's impaired vision, I was astonished that she had spotted it.

She stunned me with her next words, this time spoken with remarkable clarity.

"Jesus died on the cross."

I nodded, my heart racing. Although our small school was located in a church building, it was not a Christian school, and I had always been careful not to talk about Jesus to the students, as mandated by the school board.

I needed to make a quick decision. Would I follow the rules, or was this a God-given opportunity to share about the Saviour?

I quickly recalled a conversation I had overheard a few days ago between Lucy's mother and another parent about the challenges of attending church with a child with special needs. Easter was just around the corner. Could Lucy have recently heard the story of Jesus's death and resurrection? It felt right in my spirit to run with what I saw as an open door.

I led Lucy to a wooden bench facing the cross.

"You're right, Lucy. Jesus did die on the cross. Do you know why?"

Lucy furrowed her eyebrows, unable to articulate a response. I thought, *how can I explain this clearly in as few words as possible?* I took a deep breath and said, "Jesus died on the cross so that you and I could have a forever home with God." Lucy blinked, her long eyelashes skimming the inner surface of her glasses.

This is going to be harder than I thought. How do you explain to a child who has intellectual challenges something even adults don't seem to grasp? I tried again. "God doesn't want people to do bad things. So, He sent His Son Jesus to earth to help people do good things." I paused to let my words sink in. Lucy blinked some more.

I pressed on. "When Jesus was on the cross, He took all the bad stuff people have ever done and made it go away, just like that -" I snapped my fingers, "- when He died."

Lucy brought her hands close to her eyes and tried to snap her fingers too. I couldn't help smiling, and continued. "After Jesus died, God brought Him back to life so He could return to Heaven and live with God forever. When we ask Jesus to come into our heart, He lives inside us. So, when we die, we come back to life too, so we can live with Jesus and God in their big house, forever and ever." I paused again, hoping and praying that my words made sense.

Lucy solemnly put her toys down. Her hands gripped the edge of the bench, and her little legs swung back and forth. Then, she lifted her right hand and tapped her chest. "I want Jesus here."

My heart soared. "Lucy, are you saying that you would like to ask Jesus to come into your heart?"

Lucy nodded earnestly.

So right there, in the middle of the afternoon in the middle of the school week in the middle of the church hallway, I led a child into the kingdom of believers.

Later that night, I couldn't help second-guessing myself. Did Lucy really understand?

I would like to think so. I yearn to think so. For, less than two weeks later, Lucy and her family were killed in a terrible car accident.

The entire school community mourned. Lucy didn't just have special needs. She had a special place in everyone's heart.

Of course, I was devastated. But I also felt a lift in my spirit, knowing that God's hand was in my impromptu decision to spend time alone with Lucy that day. His hand was in the placement of the cross that spurred our conversation. His hand was on me as I stepped out of my comfort zone to share the gospel with a young girl. And His hand was on little Lucy, who chose to accept Jesus into her heart, just weeks before He took her home.

I am more assured now than ever that God gives us these beautiful moments to rise up into who He has truly called us to be. During that alone time with Lucy, my identity as a teacher faded and my glorious calling to be His hands and feet on earth surged forth.

Lucy, welcome to our family.

Easter Dinner

BY IAN MCKERRACHER

The taste was incredible! Sing Jung rolled the one grain of rice around over his tongue. Back and forth, side to side, thankful that it was under-cooked so that it lasted long enough for him to enjoy its texture; feel it in his mouth…as he did every day at this joyful time. Reluctantly, Jung swallowed the single grain of rice and then looked again into the small pewter bowl that held his meal.

Supper time was his favourite time of the day. Jung smiled as he thought about that. "It's my lunch time and breakfast time, too," he said aloud to himself, though in a voice barely above a whisper.

His slight movement caused the chains to sing their distempered song at being disturbed in the gloom. Jung took another grain of rice and put it in his mouth. "Thank you, Jesus," he said quietly to his precious Cellmate. There was no question for Jung about whether Jesus had an Easter Sunday.

The Gækkebrev: A Secret Snowdrop Letter

BY CAROL L. MACKAY

As Kristen shuffled up the sidewalk to her house in her winter boots, she noticed that her favorite flowers were blooming in the flowerbed. They had broken through the icy snow. Snowdrops were her favorite flower, because when their droopy white petals appeared, it meant that winter was almost over and spring was on its way.

Kristen opened the front door and met her mother in the hallway. Her mom handed her an envelope. "This came in the mail today."

"What is it?" Kristen asked.

"That, I don't know. It's addressed to you, so I didn't open it."

Kristen opened the envelope and pulled out a piece of folded white paper. It wasn't an ordinary piece of paper, though. There were holes clipped out of the paper in the shape of hearts, flowers and triangles. It reminded her of the snowflakes she made at school at Christmas. But Christmas was long past, and it would be Easter very soon. Kristen noticed there was another interesting thing about this letter. A snowdrop flower was inserted into one of the corner holes. A poem was written on the paper. Kristen read it aloud:

I know a family of very smart fleas
who can write as well as hop.
They want to help you guess who sent
this gækkebrev and snowdrop.
The fleas have written my name below
They promised they wouldn't jump.
Guess right, you'll get a chocolate egg
I'll get one if you're stumped!

A * * * * *

M * * * *

"What is this?" Kristen handed the piece of paper to her mom.

"It's a *gækkebrev*! I haven't seen one of these since I was a young girl living in Denmark."

"A *gækkebrev*?" Kristen repeated. She'd never heard of such a thing.

"Yes, it's a Danish tradition. It's a guessing-game letter. You must try to figure out who sent it to you. If you get it right, the person who sent it will give you a chocolate egg. If not, you give them one."

Kristen took the letter up to her room. She re-read the poem. Who could have sent it? She wanted to solve the mystery. How could she learn who sent it? The sender's initials were A. M. Kristen's mom's name was Else. Her dad's name was Ichiro. All their last names began with a H. There were no A's or M's at all.

Kristen had a few friends whose last names began with M. But she didn't think they'd know what a *gækkebrev* was. Kristen couldn't think of anyone who could have sent the letter. She'd have to think harder. Who would know about this kind of letter? It would have to be someone who knew about the Danish tradition. Kristen knew only one person, other than her mom, who was Danish. But this person's last name didn't begin with an M. But her first name did! And what about the snowdrop?

Kristen smiled. Of course! "I figured it out!" she yelled as she ran down the stairs.

"Wow, that was quick," said her mom.

Kristen held out her hand. "May I borrow your phone?"

"Sure," replied her mother.

Kristen texted. "Auntie Marie, it was you!" Then she waited for a reply. Did she guess right?

Mom's phone buzzed. Kristen read the text. "You figured it out! Congratulations! I'll bring over your special prize."

Half an hour later, there was a knock on the door. Auntie Marie handed Kristen a beautiful, foil-wrapped chocolate egg. It smelled so good!

"How did you figure it out so quickly?" asked Auntie Marie.

"You fooled me with the A. M. initials, but I know you have snowdrops in your backyard, like we have in our front yard. I guessed yours must be blooming right now, too."

"I should have known you'd remember. They're your favourite flower, after all," said Auntie Marie.

"Could you show me how to make a *gækkebrev*, Auntie? I'd like to send some to my friends."

"I'd love to," said Auntie Marie. "We'll need paper, a pencil and scissors."

"And snowdrops from our garden," said Kristen. "We can't forget the snowdrops!"

How to Make a Gækkebrev or Secret Snowdrop Letter

Fold a plain white piece of paper (8 1/2″ X 11″) in half. Then fold in half again. Use your scissors to make wavy edges on the unfolded sides. Cut shapes like hearts or diamonds into the folded sides of the paper, just like you would if you were making paper snowflakes.

Open up your paper. Write Auntie Marie's poem somewhere on the paper. Do not write your name on the page. Instead, draw tiny dots on the paper: one dot for each letter in your name. You can turn these dots into "fleas" by adding little legs to the dots. If you want to make it more difficult to guess, do not provide your initials. Use only "fleas."

Place a snowdrop flower in one of the holes in your letter. Fold the letter and put it in an envelope.

Mail /deliver your Gækkebrev.

Wait and see if your friend knows it is you. If they guess, be prepared to give them a little chocolate egg. You do not have to give an egg, even though it is tradition. You can do it just for the fun of guessing, too. Use this poem if you don't want to give or get a chocolate egg:

I know a family of very smart fleas
who can write as well as hop.
They want to help you guess who sent
this Gækkebrev and snowdrop.
The fleas have written my name below
They promised they wouldn't jump.
These puzzling fleas know my name
If you don't, I guess you're stumped!

Precious Moments in an Unprecedented Time

BY SALLY MEADOWS

We were three weeks into our trip when the world turned upside down.

After months of planning, Tim and I couldn't wait to start our retirement with a cross-Canada tour in our new winterized RV. Our neighbours in Surrey thought we were crazy to leave before spring. But we had another reason to get on the road quickly: my mother-in-law, Dee, who lived in Thunder Bay, had been recently diagnosed with progressive dementia. We needed to see her, and soon.

Of course, we were aware that the novel coronavirus COVID-19 was spreading overseas. We were optimistic that, should it reach Canada, we would be perfectly safe in our well-outfitted RV.

It wasn't until we were past the Manitoba-Ontario border that we started noticing people wearing face masks. I had advocated for a TV and radio-free trip, but clearly it was time to find out what on earth was going on.

We were shocked to learn that the virus was wreaking havoc in Ontario. People were dying, and seniors were among the worst hit.

We pulled into an eerily vacant big-box store parking lot on the outskirts of Kenora to regroup. How could we have been so oblivious? Should we turn around and go home immediately?

As Dee's Power of Attorney, Tim had business to attend to on his mother's behalf, as she had recently moved into the retirement home and needed to sell her house. We'd come this far; we agreed to press on.

I called Sunshine Villa to see if we could visit. The receptionist was cool and efficient: "No visitors allowed in the building under any circumstances."

Thankfully, no one at the facility had tested positive for the virus—yet. We were told if we wore masks and stayed two metres away, we could visit Dee through her closed patio doors.

I phoned Dee to let her know we'd be in Thunder Bay that night, but wouldn't be able to come and visit her just yet.

"Oh, that's too bad," she said. "Why not?"

I raised my eyebrows and glanced over at my husband. "Your place is in lockdown, Mom. There's a pandemic going on."

"Oh, right. So where will you stay?"

"In our RV."

"I'd love to see it!"

"Mom, you're in lockdown. You can't leave."

"Oh, that's too bad. When will I see you then?"

I rubbed my forehead. "Mom, you're on the ground floor, right?"

"I think so. Oh, yes, I see a lovely patio outside."

"We can visit you, but we have to stay outside."

The drive to Thunder Bay went by quickly as Tim and I discussed our plan of action. Besides tending to business, we agreed it was important to make our time with Dee as special as possible. Once we wrapped up our responsibilities, we would head back west.

Our first stop in the city was Dee's bungalow. Although the lawn and gardens needed tending to, inside it was clean and sparsely furnished. The company we had hired to help Dee downsize prior to her move had done an excellent job.

I phoned Dee to let her know we had arrived and would contact her the next day. It was almost nightfall, and we were bone tired.

In the morning I called the Villa to see if we could drop off some gifts for Dee. They assured us they would take care of disinfection. Thankfully, the receptionist gave us the number of a local seamstress who made cloth masks, as they were impossible to find in stores.

I picked up the masks, found a florist with curb-side service, dropped by Bulk Barn for two boxes of gluten-free cookies, and contacted a real estate agent. After dropping her gifts off outside the reception doors, Tim and I returned to Dee's bungalow.

After assessing the house repairs and yard work needed, Tim said, "If all goes well, I think we wrap up here by Easter weekend."

As disappointed as we were to have to abort our trip, the results of my research were unequivocal: the pandemic wasn't going anywhere soon.

After supper, we returned to the Villa. We phoned Dee as we approached her patio. It would be hard for her to recognize us while we were wearing masks.

Although we had to deal with the awkwardness of having a conversation by phone through patio doors while standing a distance away, Dee was clearly delighted by our presence and the gifts.

The next two weeks were crazy busy. Limited access to retail stores made getting Dee's property in order that much harder. But we learned to improvise with what we could get. Dee was our focus in the evenings. It was heartbreaking to witness her decline in memory, but we concentrated on treasuring our time together as family.

When Dee lamented she missed going to church—Sunday morning services had shut down—Tim brought his guitar so we could sing hymns together. Sometimes we could hear the other residents joining in. We prayed together too—for the safety of the residents, and for an end to the crisis.

The Thursday before Easter, we handed the house keys over to the real estate agent. We dropped off a small bottle of grape juice, package of miniature crackers, and a shot-glass-sized plastic cup for Dee in anticipation of our time together the next day.

On Good Friday, we each read a verse from Matthew 26:26-28 while celebrating communion together/apart. I could see the raw emotions on Dee's face, and could only imagine what was going through her mind. I ached to hug her.

On Saturday Tim and I got ready for our trip home. We worked quietly, each lost in our own thoughts. I was pretty sure Tim was thinking the same thing as me: tomorrow could very well be the last time we would ever see Dee.

Easter is a time of celebration, and we were determined to make our final hours with Dee as joyful as possible. As we lifted our voices together in praise, I couldn't help hoping that, just as Jesus's death and resurrection had led to new life for all, our post-pandemic world would be, on all counts, infinitely better than the one that we unexpectedly left behind.

As we made our way back to the RV, I turned and waved, tears blurring my vision. None of us knew what lay ahead. But I felt peace in my heart knowing that I would remember this time not by what we'd lost, but by the precious moments gained.

Mr. Nobody's Easter Surprise

BY DIANE WELCH

In a little yellow house, in the wee hours of the morning, Mr. Nobody was preparing his coffee. He had his favourite blue mug all warmed up. Soon he would wake everyone, but first he had to meet his friend the Easter Bunny. The Easter Bunny had texted Mr. Nobody and told him he would meet him outside in the front garden.

Mr. Nobody opened the front door to see his handsome friend the Easter Bunny. He stood six feet tall to the tip of his long fluffy ears, had huge bright blue eyes, a white fluffy cotton tail, huge feet, long whiskers that jetted out in all directions and had a cute little bright pink nose! He was smartly dressed in a yellow plaid vest, blue pants and a bright purple bow tie. Mr. Nobody gave his friend a huge hug.

Mr. Nobody and the Easter Bunny started to hide the colourful eggs in the trees, bushes and flower gardens. Then they went quietly into the house. There they hid more eggs so that Austin, Hope, Page and Katie would be very busy looking for chocolate eggs.

Illustration by Dave Welch

Mr. Nobody had an idea. He decided to unwrap the foil, for this could be a fire hazard, and place the chocolate eggs into a bowl and microwave the eggs together! But... it was three o clock in the morning and everyone was sleeping...

"Mr. Nobody, you can't wake up the family! That is a rule!" the Easter Bunny exclaimed.

"Oh, sorry. I'll just sit down for a bit and think where I'm going to hide the chocolate bunnies you brought."

The Easter Bunny continued hiding eggs in the bedrooms, the tub, kitchen, piano and door frames.

As Mr. Nobody rested, he drank his coffee, and had strawberry jam and toast for his morning snack. Sitting right in front of him were the chocolate bunnies. Too much temptation! You see, Mr. Nobody loves chocolate, coffee, strawberry jam - and practical jokes!

Mr. Nobody opened the containers and ate all the ears off! Then he hid the leftovers inside the piano bench. Afterward, he joined his friend and continued to hide more eggs.

Then Mr. Nobody had another idea. He filled a cup up with water, placed it on top of the shed, tied dental floss around the cup, and hung a blue egg dangling from the end.

"Oh, good one," the Easter Bunny chuckled. “I hid some golden eggs in very difficult spots, too. Now that the kids are older, they need a challenge, " he declared.

Finally, when the work was done, the Easter Bunny hopped away to the neighbours’ house. Mr. Nobody lay down in his invisible bed with his favourite blue blanket and slept.

Later in the morning after more coffee and his second breakfast, Mr. Nobody helped all four kids look for the eggs. Katie started in the living room. She went to the piano and opened the bench to see all four chocolate bunnies with their ears eaten off! She then looked up at the ceiling fan. What did she find? A golden egg!

Austin came along beside the shed and opened the shed door to find his golden egg, but he could not figure out how a blue egg was dangling from thin air. He carefully grabbed the egg and … SPLASH! Water soaked Austin from head to toe!

Hope was busy collecting eggs when she looked way up in the trees. High in a branch was a golden egg! But when Daddy got the ladder up the tree, the egg was gone! How was that possible? There sitting in the tallest branch, a cheeky squirrel had taken the golden egg.

"Looks like you are out of luck, Hope. Even the squirrels like the eggs," said Dad.

Page, in the meantime, was looking for her golden egg. Where did she find it? There on the inside of the canoe, under the bow, was a golden egg!

After all the fun, the family went to church and listened to the Easter story of Jesus. He arose from the grave and is alive! Later, they came home and had a pancake breakfast. Then they all sat on the couch together and with thankful hearts, ate their Easter treats.

Remember to keep your eyes on Jesus and be thankful for special treats along the way!

White as Snow

BY MARNIE POHLMANN

The little girl skipped out of the house into the yard. She wore a new dress, a white Easter dress. In her curly hair was a white ribbon. On her feet were white knee-high socks and polished white Mary Janes with the slightest heel that tapped when she walked on hard floors, which is why she was sent outside.

"Stay clean," Mama directed. "No hanging upside down from the cherry tree!"

Trying to be obedient, she tap-tapped her way down the paved driveway and onto the sidewalk. She twirled, enjoying how her beautiful new dress flared open like a flower blooming.

Suddenly, she was pushed from behind. She hadn't seen the bully approach. He always seemed to take pleasure in tormenting her, and she didn't know why. She was off balance from twirling when he shoved her, so she landed hard, right in a mud puddle beside the sidewalk. Thick brown water climbed onto her lap.

"Why?!" she demanded.

He shrugged his shoulders and smirked an ugly grin. "I like it," was all he would say.

"Well, I don't!" she retorted.

"So what? I'm bigger and I like it!" He laughed and walked away.

There was no tap-tapping as she shuffled back home. She knew Mama would be angry. Her new dress was ruined. She knew *she* would be the one to be punished, and *he* would not.

Opening the door, she slowly tip-toed to the kitchen where Mama was busy slicking back the rooster tail above her brother's pouting face. Mama turned to look at her.

"We're not quite ready to go yet, honey. Go back outside for a bit more."

Mama didn't notice the ugly stains? She looked down at herself, confirming the mud did show. But all Mama did was give her a hug and steer her gently back outside. Outside where the bully was.

He was back, standing beside another mud puddle. Where had the mud come from? Before she had only noticed blue sky, birds singing in the trees, the green grass, and the start of spring flowers in Mama's garden. But sure enough, muddy water rested in pools throughout the neighbourhood.

She watched as he jumped in one, glorying at how the mud sprayed up around him. He hadn't noticed her yet, but his splashing threw up more mud. This time it reached her face and hair ribbon.

He seemed to be having so much fun jumping in the mud, and Mama had not even noticed the stains on her. *And he's just going to push me into the mud again anyway*, she reasoned to herself.

She stepped into the nearest puddle and sat down. She gathered mud around her, bathing in the dirt to cover herself before he threw more at her. She knew it was wrong. She knew she was ruining her pretty Easter dress. Yet somehow, she liked the squish of mud as it seeped inside her shoes when she stood up to run from puddle to puddle. The tap-tapping had turned to squelch-squelching.

"Let's go," called Mom. Climbing into the back seat of the station wagon, she huddled against the far door, expecting at any moment that a brother would tattle about her being so dirty.

No one noticed her, though. She was confused. Wasn't the sight and stench of the mud obvious? Couldn't they see it covering everything?

At the Easter church service, she saw the other girls, all dressed in new dresses, soft shades of pink and green and white.

"If I stand beside them someone will certainly notice how dirty I am," she thought, so she stayed close to her mom, trying to hide in the shadows.

In the sermon, the minister described how the Jews had been slaves for hundreds of years in Egypt, and how God told them to mark their doors with the blood of a pure lamb.

"God said, 'Eat standing up, with your coat on, ready to leave for the Promised Land.'"

She remembered the story from Sunday School. The Angel of Death came that night to kill the oldest boy in each house, but not in the houses marked with blood. The blood showed the angel all the families who believed God could and would rescue them.

The minister then described the week leading up to the death of Jesus on the cross. How Jesus was beaten, with blood pouring over his face from a wretched thorny crown forced onto his head. And then they put him on the cross to die. The minister paused and turned to the wooden cross hanging on the wall behind him. It was draped with a black cloth. She looked down at her dress and saw the mud had dried to a colour that matched the cloth on the cross. The minister pointed to the cloth and her eyes grew wide as he looked directly at her.

"That black cloth is *your* sin," he exclaimed. "The sin of history, the sin that has been thrown at you through circumstances, and the sin you have chosen yourself."

She lowered her eyes in shame. Tears streaked over the mud on her cheeks. She wiped her eyes, trying to wash her face but knew she was just mixing the dirt around more. She quietly tried to wipe her face on her short puffy sleeves, but the material was already soaked through with dirt and wasn't helping at all. Being sorry was not enough.

The minister's voice had become quiet and she looked up to see him draping another cloth over the black one. This cloth was a deep red. He made sure it covered every bit of the black cloth.

"You don't have to stay in sin. Remember the blood of the lambs at Passover? It was the blood of a sacrificed lamb painted on the door that showed the Angel of Death who believed God could rescue them. Jesus gave himself on the cross as that sacrifice, at the exact time it was needed in the world, because he was the perfect sacrifice. His blood can be poured over you just as it was on the doors so long ago. Do you believe God can and will rescue you from sin? Will you ask God to allow the sacrifice of Jesus to be accepted in your place?"

"Oh, yes," she whispered. "I would rather be covered with Jesus' blood than with all this mud. Then God will see the blood and know I believe He will rescue me."

The minister continued. “It doesn’t end there. Jesus’ blood covers the sin that keeps us from God, but then Jesus did even more. He rose from the grave. He conquered death so we can live for eternity with God. Hallelujah! Isaiah says, 'though your sin be as scarlet,' yes, even as your sin is covered with Jesus' blood, 'it will be white as snow.' Jesus' blood washes us clean. Jesus makes us white as snow so we can live in the presence of God. Do you believe?"

The minister paused as he hung another cloth over the red one. This cloth was white. It did not cover the red but seemed to be framed by the red cloth, as if tucked into and protected by the blood sacrifice.

“Only by the blood of Jesus can we live today, tomorrow, and for eternity in holiness, washed as white as snow.”

Her heart filled with wonder that God could cover her with Jesus’ blood to make her white as snow. She looked down again and fingered her lacey white Easter dress.

"Look, Mama, I'm white as snow."

PART VI
RECIPES

Photo by Marnie Pohlmann

Easter Lunch at Grandma's

BY BOBBI JUNIOR

Grandma Bertha immigrated from Wholynia, Russia as a teenager. Her family settled in the Bruderheim area of Alberta where she met and married Daniel in1919. Bertha and Daniel settled in Radway, Alberta where they raised a family of five. Eventually the family moved to Edmonton where the children could access trade school and university. Over the years, the children married and the clan grew, as did the family traditions.

Easter was a favourite for we grandkids. After Easter services at our various churches, the siblings, their spouses, and a growing number of grandchildren swarmed our grandparents' small house. Grandma would have already set out an Easter lunch of homemade rhubarb juice, cold ham with her tangy canned crabapple sauce, and best of all, her much-adored potato pancakes.

Now, I've ordered potato pancakes from numerous restaurants over the years, but none compare to Grandma's Russian style, light, delicate creations. They were, and still are a gastronomical delight.

I can still picture Grandma standing over the stove in her tiny kitchen, a green-trimmed, flowered apron covering her best Easter dress. All we could see was her back as she prepared an unending supply of potato pancakes while her children, their spouses, and we grandchildren devoured them.

I wonder if Grandma ever sat down to eat some herself? I have no memory of that.

I do remember the recipe, though. When I married and our children came along, potato pancakes, Russian style, became part of our Easter tradition as well. Our kids are adults now, but if I mention I made potato pancakes a nostalgic look softens their faces, quickly followed by, "Did you save some for me?"

BERTHA'S POTATO PANCAKES - Russian style

1. Stir together in a large bowl in the following order:

- 5 cups grated potatoes. The potatoes can be peeled or scrubbed. 2 large russet potatoes will give about 5 cups grated. If you don't have russets, substitute whatever you have on hand.
- 4 eggs, beaten lightly with a fork
- 2 cups milk
- 1 cup white flour
- 1 teaspoon salt

2. Prep the pans

- I use two or three small skillets at a time to make round pancakes. If you use a large skillet, make your pancakes an oval shape.
- Turn burners to medium heat
- Set the pans on the burners and let them warm up for 2 minutes

3. Cooking

- Add about 1/2 teaspoon of butter to each pan. Butter is

much tastier than margarine or oil, but those will work as well.

- Pour 1/4 cup batter into the pan and spread it thin with the back of a spoon
- Cook 1 - 2 minutes on the first side. It will look almost dry on top, and be a golden brown on the bottom.
- Flip, and cook about 1 minute on the second side
- Stir the batter each time you dip in for another ¼ cup
- The last bit of batter will be mostly liquid. I use a slotted spoon get the last of the potatoes, and drizzle some of the liquid over top as needed.

Makes about 18 pancakes, 6 inches wide.

Serve with butter and ketchup, or applesauce.

TIPS

- Being clever and modern, I once tried shredding the potatoes in a food processer. It may have been modern, but it wasn't clever. They didn't come out at all the same.
- Grandma had the men and the big kids grate the potatoes. Now that was clever!

4. To freeze:

- Cool pancakes thoroughly in a single layer on racks
- Place racks in the freezer for 30 minutes so the pancakes don't stick together when frozen
- Store in an air-tight container or freezer bag
- Take out as many as you need when you need them

Many thanks to Grandma Bertha for the thousands of potato pancakes I'm sure she made over the years.

Golden Carrot Soup

CONTRIBUTED BY VALERIE RONALD

1/4 cup butter
1 medium onion, diced
1 clove garlic, minced
5 cups water
2 ½ cups peeled, sliced carrots
1/4 cup long grain white rice
2 Tbsp. chicken bouillon mix
½ tsp. salt, or to taste
1 – 2 Tbsp. chopped fresh parsley or 1 Tbsp. dried parsley

Melt butter in large saucepan. Sauté onion and garlic until tender. Add water, carrots, rice and bouillon mix. Bring to a boil. Cover and simmer 20 to 25 minutes until carrots are tender. Cool completely before pouring into blender, part at a time. Cover and blend until smooth, or use immersion blender in saucepan. Add salt and parsley. Reheat, if necessary. Serves 4. Amounts can be tripled to make six 4 cup portions to freeze.

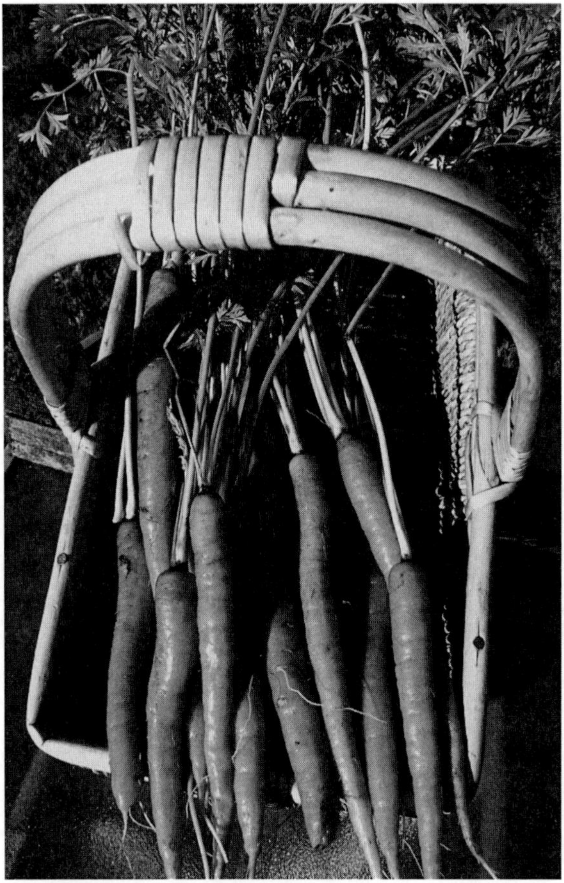

Photo by Valerie Ronald

Slow Cooker Easter Ham

CONTRIBUTED BY LORRAINE BAYCROFT

1 cured, bone-in picnic ham
1 cup light brown sugar
1 cup fresh pineapple juice
4-6 slices canned pineapple
½ cup maple syrup
1 tsp. salt
1 Tbsp. black pepper

Place the ham in the slow cooker with the flat side down. Sprinkle salt, pepper, and brown sugar over the ham, rubbing it in. Add the pineapple juice and maple syrup. Arrange the pineapple slices on top and on the sides of the ham. Cook on high for 3-5 hours or low for 6-8 hours. Remove ham from the slow cooker and let it sit for 10-15 minutes before slicing.

Turnip Puff

CONTRIBUTED BY VALERIE RONALD

6 cups peeled turnip, cubed
2 Tbsp. butter
2 eggs, beaten
3 Tbsp. all-purpose flour
1 Tbsp. brown sugar
1 tsp. baking powder
3/4 tsp. salt
1/8 tsp. ground black pepper
nutmeg, a pinch
1/2 cup bread or Panko crumbs
2 Tbsp. melted butter

Boil turnip until tender. Drain and mash well. Add butter and egg and mix well. (this can be done a day ahead) Combine flour, brown sugar, baking powder, salt, pepper and nutmeg. Stir into turnip mixture. Place in a buttered casserole dish. Combine bread crumbs and melted butter and sprinkle on top. Bake uncovered at 375° F. for 20 minutes or until bread crumbs are golden brown. Serves 6.

Hot Cross Buns

CONTRIBUTED BY LORRAINE BAYCROFT

Scald 1 cup of milk with 1 cup of raisins. Add ¾ cup margarine. When the margarine is melted add ½ cup chopped mixed peel.

In a bowl, put 1 ¾ cups warm water, a pinch of ginger and 2 tsp. sugar. Add 2 Tbsp. quick-rising yeast and 1 cup of flour. Mix well and let sit until it starts to bubble.

Combine 2 above mixtures. Add ¾ cup sugar and 1 ½ tsp salt. Beat well, then beat in 4 eggs, one at a time.

Stir in 1 more cup of flour along with 1 ½ tsp. cinnamon, ½ tsp. nutmeg, and 1 capful of lemon essence or 1 Tbsp. of grated lemon rind.

Now add enough flour to knead into a soft, pliable dough.

. . .

Let sit for 15 minutes. Punch down. Leave 15 minutes. Make into buns. Let rise to double and bake.

Decorate with icing crosses when cool.

Lovella's Paska

BY PAT GERBRANDT

My mother did not bake Paska, so I had no favourite recipe until I learned of this one!

Photo by Pat Gerbrandt

Set to soften:
2 Tbsp. active dry yeast
1 tsp. sugar
1 cup warm water

Let stand about 10 minutes, until yeast rises.

Wash and zest or peel very thinly, using a sharp knife or vegetable peeler:

- 1 medium lemon
- 1 medium orange

Remove the seeds and white pith. Place fruit and zest in a blender or food processor.

Add:

- 1 ¼ cup milk, warmed
- ½ cup butter, melted (no substitute)
- 2 large eggs
- ¾ cup sugar
- 1 tsp. salt

Process until mixture is smooth. Pour into a large mixing bowl or the bowl of your stand mixer, together with the softened yeast.

Add flour, 1 cup at a time, using

- 6-7 cups all-purpose flour

Mix well, adding flour very gradually until the dough is easily handled. It should still be soft, not stiff. (I use disposable gloves for kneading; this makes it easier to finish a dough and not have it stick to my hands.)

Cover the dough with a cloth or plastic wrap and set to rise until doubled. This could take 1 – 1.5 hours. Punch down the dough, let it rest 10-60 minutes, then shape as you prefer. I like the rounded top-loaf, made by putting a ball of dough in a tin can. Parchment paper is great for lining the can or any baking pan.

Cover and let it rise until doubled. This dough rises significantly, so make small buns or loaves!

Preheat the oven to 350° F. and bake 12-20 minutes, watching carefully not to bake the Paska too long. Cool baking pans on racks. Freeze as soon as the bread is cool, or ice with your favourite white frosting* and sprinkle with coloured sugar if desired.
*A simple glaze, cream cheese frosting, or pudding frosting
(Ingredient list used with permission from Lovella Schellenberg of "Mennonite Girls Can Cook")

PART VII
BIOGRAPHIES

Photo by Lynn J. Simpson

Biographies

Anderson, Alan

Alan lives in Deroche, B.C. with his wife, Terry. His overall writing theme is "Touched by grief, held by hope." Co-author of *Good Grief People* by Angel Hope Publishing, 2017. Four stories published in *Story by Story: The Power Of a Writer,* Unstoppable Writers Publishing, Nov. 2018. Blog: https://scarredjoy.ca. "Writing as Healing" series of articles for FellowScript magazine 2020; Member of InScribe since 2014.

Arseneault, Normand

Normand and his wife Deborah are ordained ministers who have served in various ministry roles. They are currently developing a writing/teaching ministry with a focus on preparing a people for the return of the Lord. More articles from the author can be found at www.highwayinthewilderness.com.

Atchison, Bruce

Bruce Atchison is a legally-blind Canadian freelance writer and author. He has written professionally for more than 20 years. His articles have appeared in a wide range of publications, from glossy magazines to photocopied underground newsletters. Atchison has also authored three paperback memoirs titled *When a Man Loves a Rabbit, Deliverance from Jericho,* and *How I Was Razed*. Additionally, he publishes blog posts three times a week on Blogspot and Wordpress. He previously dabbled in electronic music, videos of which are up on YouTube. Atchison lives in the perfect writing environment, a blink-and-you-miss-it hamlet in northern Alberta.

Bancroft, Lorraine

Lorraine Baycroft started cooking and baking for her family when she was a teenager. With both parents working, Lorraine would come home from school and put on dinner.

Lorraine has been married nearly 63 years and enjoys baking, sewing, knitting, petit point, gardening, needle work, and puzzles. Her daughter, Author Diane Welch, pleaded with her Mom to share some of these delicious family treats for the Easter Analogy Book. We are blessed she did just that!

Barclay, Susan

Susan Barclay writes from southwestern Ontario where she lives with her husband, young adult daughter and their Boston Terrier. Her short stories, personal experience stories and articles have been published in various anthologies and magazines and she is a regular contributor to InScribe Writers Online. In addition to writing, Susan enjoys reading, travel, hiking, and encouraging others. For further information please visit www.susan-barclay.blogspot.com

Dove, Lynn

Lynn Dove is an award-winning author and free-lance writer with articles published in several magazines and anthologies. Her blog, "Journey Thoughts" has a world-wide following and is a Canadian Christian Writing Award winner. She lives in Cochrane, AB., with her husband and dotes on her grandbabies every chance she gets!

Earl, Patricia

Patricia has been writing short articles and poems for many years. Some have been published in magazines and anthologies. Patricia is the devotional editor of *Eternal Ink*, an on line e-zine and earlier this year published her first book *Chosen By Grace*. She has been a member of Inscribe Christian Writers' Fellowship for many years. Patricia lives with her husband Brian, has three children, five grandchildren and three great-grandchildren. Her hobbies are quilting, crocheting and gardening. She is an elder at her church and plays the keyboard in the church praise team.

Enns, L. Marie

L. Marie Enns is a retired teacher, but an unretired writer. She is a long-time member of InScribe Christian Writers' Fellowship. She writes mostly poetry and devotionals, and has published three books. Currently, she and three friends write the "Meditation Moment" column for the newspaper of her hometown in Saskatchewan. She has also enjoyed serving as church librarian, Ladies' Bible Study leader, and gospel singer.

Marie and her husband, Henry, have one single and three married children, but one daughter-in-law went to be with the Lord in 2016. The family also includes five grandchildren, (two married,) and one great-grandchild.

Ens, Alvin

Teacher, prose writer, poet, writing mentor

To essay is to try. A wise old teacher once told a young buck, me, never to assign a piece of writing whose type I had not tried. I have essayed to live by that dictum. Over the years, I have tried poetry, fiction, creative non-fiction, history, family history, Christian apologetics, humour, and many personal remembrances, often a mixed blend of essay types. My articles, some are published and some unpublished, some fact, some fiction, some fancy and some almost-true.

Espe, Sylvia Engen

Sylvia Engen Espe was blessed to have been born into a Christian home in southern Saskatchewan in 1928. She has many cherished memories of a happy childhood living on a farm, attending a rural school, and active in a church that was the centre of her social life. Sylvia, retired from an extensive career in heath care, now appreciates her children, grandchildren, and thirteen great grandchildren. Her many interests include handcrafts, writing, and photography. She presently enjoys living in Camrose, Alberta, but remains loyal to Saskatchewan. She thanks God for His presence on her journey through life.

Espeseth, Sharon
Having always loved children, Sharon Espeseth chose a teaching career. Several years later, she married Hank. Together they raised three children, adopted as infants. When their kids were 10, 11, and 12 years, they moved to a small farm. Farming was a new experience for all but Hank, who had grown up on a nearby farm. The rest of them, in training, gained new knowledge, skills and perspectives. Awed by her surroundings and watching their teens adapt to country life, awakened Sharon's writing muse. Her essays, stories and poems soon appeared in farm, faith and city newspapers plus various anthologies.

Faire, Jocelyn
Jocelyn Faire describes herself as a reluctant author with a hope filled story to tell. Her first book, *Who is Talking Out of My Head?* chronicles her journey of grief after the tragic accident that took the lives of her two young adult children and a future daughter-in-law. Her second book *In the Becoming,* (carrying on after life derails) was published with Siretona Creative in November of 2020. She studied Creative Writing at the University of Calgary. She sporadically maintains her blog: https://whoistalking.wordpress.com
She delights in grand-mothering, kayaking, beauty and world travels. Contact her at jbmarietalking@gmail.com

Fast-Vlaar, Angelina
Angelina's family immigrated from Holland shortly after WWII. After marrying Peter Fast and raising a family of five, she had the privilege to teach Psychology courses at Niagara College in Welland, ON. Articles, poems and non-fiction stories have been published in several magazines as well as in the *Hot Apple Cider*

series. She has authored four books - recounting her memories of WWII, her saga with cancer, the loss of her first husband in the Australian outback, and her caregiver journey as she walked with her second husband during his struggle with dementia. Angelina makes her home in St. Catharines, Ontario. www.angelinafast.com

Ford, Denise
Denise grew up in a little town in Pennsylvania, at a time when wandering by yourself from dewy morning to firefly evening wasn't a risk, but a reality. The only one in her Girl Scout troop to earn the Writer's Badge, she began a lifetime journey seeking to use words to inspire others. Married to a Canadian, she now lives near Calgary, Alberta. She juggles her time between caring for her grandchildren and carving out time to write. You can view her inspirational reflections at www.walkingwithdustyanddee.com

Gerbrandt, Pat
Pat Gerbrandt enjoyed reading from early childhood, but the possibility of writing took her by surprise at midlife. Her husband, Gerald, encouraged her to attend a Manitoba Christian Writers Association seminar in 1982, and she has not stopped learning. She has written devotionals (The Upper Room), house and design articles, community news, and features for local magazines and papers. She does copy editing and a bit of developmental editing. Pat and her husband live in Steinbach, where they enjoy watching birds in their backyard – when they're not reading! Walking, and cycling (when the snow is gone) make exploring enjoyable. They always feel honoured when any of their three children (all married) or seven grandchildren can visit. Pat has just revived her blog, patgwriter.wordpress.com

Guenter, Lorilee
Lorilee Guenter lives in Saskatoon, Sk. She enjoys hiking and exploring random country roads with her husband. The sights, sounds and smells of nature remind her of God's abundance and

power. Inspiration for her writing and art come from these hikes as well as many easily overlooked moments of life.
Lorilee Guenter lori@untroubled.org
My Fragmented Journey: http://www.untroubled.org/lori

Guest, Gloria L.
Gloria L. Guest is a past newspaper reporter, where she covered local, provincial and national news. She has also contributed to various newspapers as a lifestyle columnist. She prefers to write memoir, creative non-fiction, blog posts, devotionals and some fiction. Currently she is working towards obtaining her Editing Certificate from Simon Fraser University while still pursuing writing interests.

Harrison, Carol
Carol Harrison is a storyteller, published author, and inspirational speaker who is passionate about helping people of all ages and abilities find their voice and reach their fullest potential. She enjoys encouraging others to tell their stories and use their God-given gifts. Carol lives in Saskatoon, SK and is a wife, mother, grandmother, and great-grandmother who enjoys family time, reading, and scrapbooking. Her grandchildren challenge her to try new avenues of writing and encourage her along the way. You can contact her at carol@carolscorner.ca

Inglis, Connie
Connie Mae Inglis is a missionary with Wycliffe Bible Translators who now lives in Edmonton, having spent much of the last 25 years in Southeast Asia with her husband and children, serving as a literacy specialist, teacher, and editor—always with a focus on helping minority language groups. She's passionate about Jesus and seeing Him in daily life, about art, both on canvas and in words, and about family, particularly her grandchildren. Connie has had both poetry and short stories published and hopes to have a novel

published within the year. Follow her on her website: conniemaeinglis.ca

Jantzen, Caran

Author of *Grow. Cook. Eat. Share. A Memoir*, Caran Jantzen and her family live in Abbotsford, BC. When not working around the homestead, Caran can be found entertaining family and friends while serving up their homegrown food. Caran enjoys writing prose by day and poetry by moonlight.
https://www.caranjantzenwrites.com/

Jones, Bob

Bob Jones is a recovering perfectionist, who collects Coca-Cola memorabilia and drinks Iced Tea. He served churches as a pastor in Ontario, Quebec and Alberta over four decades and now is a coach to pastors and church boards across Canada.
A master communicator, Bob is making his mark as the author of a best-selling, award winning book, *Ornament*, and two others. He recently added ghostwriting to his resume and is in partnership with Barking Dog Publishing to share stories of inspiring Canadians. Bob is happily married to Jocelyn for 41 years, a father of two accomplished sons and a proud grandfather of five.

Junior, Bobbi

Bobbi Junior's passion was to use story to show how God brings value for our suffering. Through memoir, Bobbi explored caregiving, grief, disability, and other life experiences, told with an honest sharing of mistakes made and victories won. Visit Bobbi's blog at www.bobbijunior.com to download samples of her award winning publications: a chapter of *The Reluctant Caregiver*, or her short story, *Tell Me About Today*. Also available is the complete serialized version of her book, *When the Bough Breaks*.

Laycock, Marcia Lee
Marcia writes from Central Alberta where she lives with her pastor/husband. Her writing began in the attic of her parents' home where she wrote poetry and stories for her dolls. They didn't complain so she kept it up. Her poetry and fiction have won various awards.

Lynn, Allison
Allison Lynn has the heart of a storyteller. Whether in her early work as an actor, or in her current role as singer, songwriter, worship leader, blogger, and band manager, Allison is drawn to the power of story to grow hearts and communities. Allison and her husband, Gerald Flemming, form the award-winning duo, Infinitely More.
This prolific duo is currently recording their 9th studio album. Infinitely More has been nominated for 15 national awards, including winning two Covenant Awards from GMA Canada. Their nationally touring ministry travels over 40,000 KM annually, serving churches of all denominations. www.InfinitelyMore.ca

MacDonald, Wendy L.
Wendy L. Macdonald is an inspirational blogger and podcaster who loves to photograph nature on Vancouver Island. Besides writing and gardening, Wendy also enjoys hiking with her husband. She homeschooled their three children and believes years of reading classics aloud developed her love of storytelling. She hopes you'll visit her "Daily Bread" style Facebook, Twitter, or Instagram. Her byline is: "My faith is not shallow because I've been rescued from the deep." Her main website is wendylmacdonald.com where she enjoys interacting with readers.

MacKay, Carol L.
Carol L. MacKay's poems and stories for children have been published in numerous magazines, including *Clubhouse Jr., Highlights, Pockets, Primary Treasure, Our Canada,* and *Kids' Ark*. Her first picture book for children, *Lily in the Loft*, about a young aspiring writer who sends a poem to the Western Producer's YC Pages, was a finalist in the Next Generation Independent Book Awards in 2019. Carol often writes about her Danish roots. "The Gækkebrev" was inspired by her Aunt Marie, who sent a gækkebrev to Canada from Denmark many years ago. Carol lives in Qualicum Beach, BC.

McKerracher, Ian
Ian is a retired tradesman and in into his second career as a speaker of a Christian organization that teaches the Christian Worldview to churches and Christians. He has been writing blogs for Faith Beyond Belief for a couple of years and is working on his first book. He has one wife, two kids, and eight grandchildren and lives in the Edmonton area of Canada.

Matchett, Eunice
Eunice Matchett is Cynde, David, and Lance's mom, Sonia and Ramona's stepmom and Grammy to eleven. Beyond her family, she is an award-winning author. Words are her tools, and the world is her workshop. Without mercy, she manipulates her reader's emotions until she has them believing what they formerly thought impossible. Those close to Eunice choose their words and actions with care, for no one knows what will end up on pages of her manuscripts. This past year she published two novels, *Beyond the Purple Sky* and *Behind her Name*.

Meadows, Sally
Sally Meadows is an award-winning author, a national award-nominated singer/songwriter, and avid photographer. Over the past eight years, she has been shortlisted for her books, stories, songs,

and blogs; been published in anthologies, magazines, and newspapers; published five children's books; oversaw the production and editing of a previous InScribe anthology; spoken at workshops and conferences; released two studio CDs and a single; and won several writing contests and national writing awards. Sally continues to challenge herself by broadening her artistic pursuits through the written word, music, photography, and other media.

Morey, Nina Faye

Nina Faye Morey is a freelance writer, editor, and speaker from Saskatoon, SK. She's had fiction, nonfiction, poetry, and art published in Christian, secular, and literary journals. She has contributed to two previous InScribe anthologies, *7 Essential Habits of Christian Writers* and *Christmas: Stories & More.* Nina's served as both columns editor and editor-in-chief for InScribe's *FellowScript* magazine. She's found working with writers extremely rewarding. She also contributes to the InScribe Writers Online Blog, and you can find her "*Refreshing Your Creativity*" at https://writerinkwell.weebly.com/. She has a B.A. in Sociology and a B.Ed. in English from the University of Saskatchewan. She's also received her Advanced Communicator Gold and Competent Leader Awards from Toastmasters. Recently widowed, Nina cherishes spending time with her children and grandchildren. When not writing, she enjoys reading, walking, and travelling.

Payne, Kimberley

Kimberley Payne is a motivational speaker and an award-winning author and a member of The Word Guild and Inscribe Christian Writer's Fellowship. Her writing relates raising a family, pursuing a healthy lifestyle and everyday experiences to building a relationship with God. Kimberley, who lives near Toronto, Canada, offers practical, guilt-free tips on improving spiritual and physical health. She believes that exercise is to the body what prayer is to the spirit and healthy eating is to the body what Bible study is to the spirit. You can visit her website at www.kimberleypayne.com

Pohlmann, Marnie

Marnie Pohlmann enjoys playing with words and Lego. She creatively and transparently shares about God's light shining in dark times. Marnie writes from northern British Columbia where she provides administrative support to our Canadian heroes in red serge and joins her husband in pastoring Taylor's Peace Community Church. She regularly contributes to *Inscribe Writers Online*, has published articles and poetry in various online and print magazines, and has spoken at ladies' events.

Ronald, Valerie

Valerie Ronald lives in Portage la Prairie, Manitoba. A graduate of Vancouver's Langara College journalism program, she has worked as a newspaper reporter, freelance writer, public speaker and bookstore employee. A member of the Manitoba Christian Writers Association, she writes devotionals for her church bulletins and online blog. Her current book project chronicles how God's faithfulness saw her through the dark valleys of divorce and cancer. She and her husband enjoy spending time with their blended family and seven grandchildren. She is a nature photographer, water colourist, cat lover and Scrabble addict.
Her devotionals can be found at: https://scriptordeus.wordpress.com

Simpson, Lynn J.

Lynn J. Simpson understands the need for creating spaces for rest, renewal, and transformation. She's rarely without her camera, capturing breathing spaces to share. She's published Breathing Spaces: A 21-Day Journal of Rest, Reflection and Renewal and 30-Day Journal of Thankfulness, Success & Joy, and contributed to Short and Sweet Too (Grace Publishing, 2017). Read Lynn's musings on faith, hope, and love on her blog (lynnjsimpson.com).

Sketchley, Janet

Janet Sketchley is the author of the Green Dory Inn Mystery Series, the Redemption's Edge Series, and the daily devotional books *A Year of Tenacity* and *Tenacity at Christmas*. She likes her fiction with a splash of mystery and a dash of Christianity. Why leave faith out of our stories if it's part of our lives? Janet writes in Atlantic Canada, and you can find her online at janetsketchley.ca.

Snyder, Ruth L.
Ruth L. Snyder is an author, coach, and publisher. She is on a mission, determined not to let people's powerful stories go to the grave with them. She guides Christian entrepreneurs along the book-writing journey, providing a safe place for them to birth their stories. Ruth has shared her expertise on platforms like Thrive Global, Women in Publishing, Authority Magazine, The Write Coach, and Author Audience Academy. Connect with Ruth at https://ruthlsnyder.com.

Somers, Sandra
Sandra Somers is a former teacher in public schools and an instructor of English as a Second Language. She has lived in Alberta and Colombia, South America. Her devotionals and award-winning inspirational articles have appeared in such publications as *FellowScript, The Christian Communicator, The Secret Place,* and *The Upper Room Disciplines*. She is also the lead writer for the InScribe Writers Online blog. Sandra currently resides in Calgary, Alberta.

Welch, Dave
Dave Welch is a Master Multi-Award-Winning Glass Artist. He is also the Illustrator for his wife's three children's Mr. Nobody's Book Series.
Married nearly 24 years, Dave has been busy with his wife Diane raising their four children. Now seeing them grown and heading off to University, has been an amazing journey. Dave enjoys growing dahlias and a vegetable garden, dog sitting, and nature walks with family.

Welch, Diane

Diane Welch is the Author of three children's books featuring Mr. Nobody. Her husband Dave has Illustrated all of the books.
With three kids off to University and another graduating soon, life stays busy with dog sitting, soccer, and gardening. Diane has enjoyed the many facets of serving on the committee for the Easter Anthology Book. The learning curve has been educational and enjoyable.

If you have enjoyed this book, we would appreciate you leaving a review.

Connect with InScribe Christian Writers' Fellowship at https://inscribe.org and on social media:

facebook.com/CanadianWriters
twitter.com/InScribeCWF
instagram.com/inscribecwf